Doing Your Master's Dissertation

STUDENT SUCCESS

Get the skills you need to succeed!

Student Success books are essential guides for students of all levels. From how to think critically and write great essays to planning your dream career, the Student Success series helps you study smarter and get the best from your time at university.

Test yourself with practical tasks

Diagnose your strengths and weaknesses

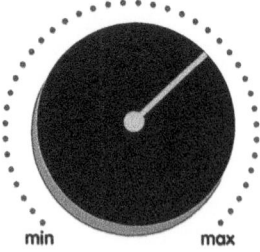

Dial up your skills for improved grades

Visit **sagepub.co.uk/study-skills**
for free tips and resources for study success

STUDENT SUCCESS

Doing Your Master's Dissertation

From Start to Finish

Inger Furseth &
Euris Larry Everett

Los Angeles | London | New Delhi
Singapore | Washington DC | Melbourne

Los Angeles | London | New Delhi
Singapore | Washington DC

SAGE Publications Ltd
1 Oliver's Yard
55 City Road
London EC1Y 1SP

SAGE Publications Inc.
2455 Teller Road
Thousand Oaks, California 91320

SAGE Publications India Pvt Ltd
B 1/I 1 Mohan Cooperative Industrial Area
Mathura Road
New Delhi 110 044

SAGE Publications Asia-Pacific Pte Ltd
3 Church Street
#10-04 Samsung Hub
Singapore 049483

Editor: Katie Metzler
Assistant editor: Anna Horvai
Production editor: Ian Antcliff
Copyeditor: Solveig Gardner Servian
Proofreader: Sharika Sharma
Marketing manager: Catherine Slinn
Cover design: Naomi Robinson
Typeset by: C&M Digitals (P) Ltd, Chennai, India
Printed and bound by Ashford Colour Press Ltd.

© Inger Furseth and Euris Larry Everett 2013

First published 2013

Apart from any fair dealing for the purposes of research or private study, or criticism or review, as permitted under the Copyright, Designs and Patents Act, 1988, this publication may be reproduced, stored or transmitted in any form, or by any means, only with the prior permission in writing of the publishers, or in the case of reprographic reproduction, in accordance with the terms of licences issued by the Copyright Licensing Agency. Enquiries concerning reproduction outside those terms should be sent to the publishers.

Library of Congress Control Number: 2012947684

British Library Cataloguing in Publication data

A catalogue record for this book is available from the British Library

ISBN 978-1-4462-6398-3
ISBN 978-1-4462-6399-0 (pbk)

Contents

List of figures viii
About the authors ix
Preface x
Introduction xi

1 Help! How do I find a research topic? 1
  1.1 Finding a topic 2
  1.2 Developing a topic 5
  1.3 Research ethics 10
  1.4 Writing a research proposal 11
  1.5 Project planning 13
  1.6 Summary 14
  1.7 Action plan 16

2 Overcoming barriers and getting started 17
  2.1 Writing blocks 18
  2.2 Processing information and making decisions 20
  2.3 The motivation to write 21
  2.4 Getting started 23
  2.5 Summary 25
  2.6 Action plan 25

3 Basic rules of writing 27
  3.1 Some rules for good writing 27
  3.2 Writing styles 30
  3.3 Structure 31
  3.4 Tricks to continue writing 35
  3.5 Summary 36
  3.6 Action plan 37

4 Who can help you? Establishing support networks 39
  4.1 Social media 39
  4.2 Students 40

4.3	The advisor	42
4.4	The responsibilities of advisors and students	42
4.5	Summary	46
4.6	Action plan	46

5 A guide for searching the literature — 47
5.1	Why search the literature?	47
5.2	How to use the literature in your thesis	48
5.3	Where to begin and what to include	50
5.4	Surf on top or dive into the deep Web?	51
5.5	Methods for searching literature	51
5.6	Bibliographic databases	54
5.7	Different types of literature	58
5.8	Identifying useful books and articles	66
5.9	How to keep a search log	68
5.10	A few useful websites	69
5.11	Summary	71
5.12	Action plan	72

6 Reviewing research literature — 73
6.1	Coherence	73
6.2	Reviewing the literature	75
6.3	Critical analysis – questions and critique	77
6.4	Critical analysis – discussing the literature	82
6.5	Evaluating arguments	86
6.6	Summary	87
6.7	Action plan	88

7 How do I formulate research questions? — 89
7.1	Research questions in quantitative and qualitative theses	90
7.2	Overall research questions	92
7.3	The rationale of the questions	96
7.4	Specified questions	98
7.5	Adjustments during the research process	100
7.6	Summary	101
7.7	Action plan	101

8 Easier said than done – choosing a suitable research design and method — 102
8.1	What is a research method?	103
8.2	Useful strategies for designing a master's thesis	104
8.3	Practical and ethical considerations when collecting data	106

    8.4 Writing the methods chapter   111
    8.5 Summary   117
    8.6 Action plan   118

9 The art of keeping a steady course – structuring the analysis   **119**
    9.1 Organizing and preparing the data for analysis   120
    9.2 Describing and interpreting the data   122
    9.3 Critical analysis of the data – developing the argument   125
    9.4 Structure   128
    9.5 Coherence   129
    9.6 Inclusive and bias-free writing   129
    9.7 Summary   130
    9.8 Action plan   131

10 Beginning and end – introduction and conclusion   **132**
    10.1 The introduction   132
    10.2 The conclusions chapter   133
    10.3 Summary   134
    10.4 Action plan   135

11 Chaos and order – editing and referencing   **136**
    11.1 A classic thesis structure   136
    11.2 Quotations   138
    11.3 Notes   139
    11.4 References   139
    11.5 Referencing in the text   141
    11.6 Referencing electronic sources   142
    11.7 List of references   143
    11.8 Summary   143
    11.9 Action plan   144

12 When is it finished? Checklist summary   **145**
    12.1 Reading the thesis with a critical eye   145
    12.2 Comments and approval from your advisors   148
    12.3 Work in progress   148

References   150
Index   153

List of figures

Figure 1.1 Initial mind map   7

Figure 1.2 Concepts from initial mind map developed into
            a more specific study   8

Figure 1.3 Gantt chart for the first semester of doing
            a master's thesis   16

Figure 2.1 Model for decision making   20

About the authors

Inger Furseth, Dr. polit, is a sociologist and professor at the University of Oslo, Norway and research associate at University of Southern California. She has written several articles and books, such as *From Quest for Truth to Being Yourself: Religious Change in Life Stories* (2006), and co-authored *An Introduction to the Sociology of Religion: Classical and Contemporary Perspectives* (2006). She has developed and taught several courses on research design and writing for students and faculty at the University of Oslo and other Norwegian universities and colleges.

Euris L. Everett, MA, has a BA with a major in teaching and an MA in organizational management. Since 1977 he has developed classes and taught in the US and Norway on motivation, decision making, planning and writing. He is the director of the Career Design Institute in Santa Maria, California.

Preface

The topic of this book is how to write a master's thesis. It is a brief handbook written for the individual student. The objective is to give the social science student at a master's degree level practical advice on how to do your master's thesis from start to finish. It is directed at the student who is going to write a thesis for the first time, even if we think that students on other levels will find it useful.

This book is a co-authored effort. The idea of writing a book on doing a master's thesis came as a result of lectures and courses the authors have given, and several years of teaching and advising many master's theses. It therefore owes a great deal to those students and to other students whose theses are readily available online. Special thanks to Sally Nash, Lois Lee and Leon Moosavi who let us use their theses. An earlier version of this book was published in Norwegian in 1997 (Universitetsforlaget), updated in 2004 and revised in 2012. This version, which is translated by Inger Furseth and proofread by Euris Larry Everett, has been updated and adapted for a British audience.

We also want to thank the anonymous reviewers and our editor at Sage, Katie Metzler, for their constructive feedback and suggestions for changes. Special thanks go to Mark Janes, Social Sciences Subject Consultant, Bodleian Libraries, University of Oxford, and Ragnhild Sundsbak, Subject Librarian of Political Science at University of Oslo Library, who have helped to edit and update the information in Chapter 5 about search methods, bibliographic databases, types of publications and keeping a search log.

Oslo and Santa Maria, August 2012

Inger Furseth

Euris Larry Everett

Introduction

It is a well-known fact that the master's thesis functions as a bottleneck for many students. It is not so difficult to attend classes and take exams, but when it is time to start the thesis, students often feel overwhelmed. The truth is that you as a student face several new academic and personal challenges. This book addresses and discusses both aspects of the writing process.

Writing a thesis requires certain skills. It seems that it is expected that master's-level students either have these skills or that they are able to develop them on their own. After teaching research design and writing at master's level for several years, we believe that many students face some of the same challenges during this phase. Writing a thesis has some personal and social challenges in addition to the academic ones. For example, many students experience a fear of writing and struggle with motivation and decision making. These issues are seldom addressed in class or in books on writing theses. We want to try to help you deal with some of these problems. What do you do when you are not motivated to write? Or when you feel that you lack the necessary skills to write an entire thesis? What are the basic rules of writing? How do you get started? And keep going? When you are working on your thesis, you need to establish an academic network. How do you actually go about doing this? What if the relationship with your advisor does not work? This book describes problems that many students face during the different stages of writing a thesis, and it provides practical suggestions for how to resolve them.

We have set aside a whole chapter to searching for research literature. The growth in online resources has changed and will continue to change when it comes to the amount and type of information available, and the methods used to access them. The problem for you as a student is that searching the literature quickly can give you the feeling of being an inexperienced globetrotter in a jungle. What types of publications should you look at first? What is available? What can librarians help you to find, and what can you find on the Internet yourself? How do you identify useful books and articles? This chapter discusses the difference between using search engines for finding information and using the deep Web. It gives an overview of various written and online sources, how to find them and evaluate their usefulness. Since this area is constantly changing, this book gives references to different electronic databases and websites.

We also describe and discuss the different parts of a thesis. How do you find a topic? How do you conduct a critical analysis of the research literature? How do you formulate research questions? Which issues should you consider when you are going to design your research and decide on the appropriate method? How do you actually construct a critical analysis of your data? We walk you through the different parts of the thesis and point out how to write them. We have tried to be as specific as possible. You will find information on what an argument is, what the introduction and conclusion should include, and how you should write notes and references. We also look at editing the thesis, finishing the work and submitting it. The text is filled with examples from completed master's theses from British and Norwegian universities. These examples demonstrate how other master's students have addressed the various challenges. The theses are taken from different disciplines in the social sciences, and most of them are available online.

Each chapter ends with a summary and an action plan. The summary points out important issues to remember during the phase that each chapter describes. The action plan is a resource section that features exercises and reflection/discussion questions designed to help you apply the information and work through the thesis.

Throughout the book we have attempted to point out how you can complete a master's thesis within the limitations you face as a student. Even if the social science disciplines vary as it relates to thesis requirements, there are some similarities. Our aim is not to present a single recipe for writing a thesis. We do not believe such a recipe exists. However, we want to inspire effective work with the thesis. Our hope is that the book will address many of the challenges you will face during the writing process and show you what you need to do to finish the thesis.

The book begins by addressing issues students face during the early phase of writing a thesis: deciding what to research and planning the work. Many students have to submit research proposals, and we outline the main content of such a proposal and how to write it. Since many students are writing a thesis for the first time and feel overwhelmed by the idea, we have chosen to address these issues in Chapter 2. We discuss how to deal with emotional blocks, motivation and decision making, to ways of identifying your strengths and weaknesses. A master's thesis represents a relatively large research project for a student, so we offer a few reminders of the basic rules of writing in Chapter 3 and how to improve your writing skills. Chapter 4 addresses the social aspects of the writing process, such as choosing and working with an advisor, using social media, and forming student work groups for added help and inspiration. In Chapter 5 we give advice and information about searching for literature. We present various sources of literature that can be used, how to find them and keep a search log. In Chapter 6, we proceed by focusing on different aspects of the thesis itself, doing a critical analysis of the literature and constructing the argument, before we show you how to formulate research questions in Chapter 7. This chapter is closely related to Chapter 1 on finding a topic. Many students mistakenly think that once they have found a topic, they have also formulated the research questions. Research questions constitute the main beam of the thesis and they need to be developed and specified. It is therefore a good idea to read Chapters 1 and 7 together. Since the research questions should guide the research design and methods, we have chosen to discuss these issues in Chapter 8. Thereafter, we outline the different aspects of a good analysis, how to describe the data, the importance of interpretation and how to critically analyse the data. Towards the end, we deal with the introduction and the conclusions chapter, editing, notes and references. Finally, Chapter 12 focuses on the process of finishing the work. Throughout the book, ethical issues are addressed.

It is important to know that you do not have to read this book from beginning to end to write a master's thesis. Students tend to begin at very different ends when they start to work on their theses. Each chapter is written in such a way that you can go back and forth in the text to find relevant information without having to read the entire book. We want you to use this book as a toolbox, where you find the information that is relevant for you. Feel free to go back and forth and use it according to your needs. All the references that are used in the text are, as usual, placed in the reference list at the end, with the exception of the many examples of literature in Chapter 5.

The book is directed at the social science student who is writing a thesis for the first time. We believe, however, that students at other levels as well as faculty and advisors will also find it useful.

1
Help! How do I find a research topic?

When you begin working on your master's thesis you will soon face a number of new challenges. You may ask yourself: 'How do I find a topic? How do I find a good advisor? Do I have the necessary skills for academic writing? Should I take an additional writing course? What kind of literature should I read?'. Most importantly, 'What should I do first?'. It might seem as if all of these challenges need to be solved immediately. Indeed, you should work on several aspects of your thesis simultaneously. However, you must decide and initiate a first step. We will begin by discussing a commonly accepted first step: finding the topic for your research.

Students face a variety of issues when they try to find a research topic. Some have difficulties in finding a topic because of the seeming wealth of possible research topics. This feeling is common during the early phase. Fortunately, you will quickly find that some topics appear to be more interesting than others on your list. Some students don't have difficulties finding a topic that can be developed into a research topic because they focus on an issue they feel strongly about and they want to use the thesis to confirm their beliefs rather than acquire new knowledge. Although it is a common strategy in research to pose questions on the basis of existing knowledge, this approach has an important premise, namely that the scientist is willing to be proven wrong. You must distance yourself enough from a topic to be able to consider that your research may prove you wrong. If this is difficult for you, consider tackling another topic. Always keep an open mind as it relates to the result of your research.

Some students look at the thesis as their 'life project' which will define their identities and future professional opportunities. Most likely, you will conduct several projects during your career, so this is not your sole opportunity to write. It is more helpful to look at the master's thesis as a project that will give you the opportunity to learn how to do research and write about it rather than seeing it as an 'identity' project.

And then there are the students who do not have a great interest in research. They are not driven by curiosity, but look instead at the thesis as a necessity to finish their degree. It is difficult to write a thesis with this attitude. If this is a description that fits you, try to look at the thesis as a source of new learning and insight. You might be surprised.

Every student has a different point of departure when it comes to finding a research topic. It is impossible to provide a detailed guide of how to go about it, but we will offer some ideas and advice that hopefully will be useful during this phase.

1.1 Finding a topic

Interest

What do you do if you are unable to come up with any ideas? Clearly, you are unlikely to achieve much success if you pick a topic that does not interest you. Which topic would you consider working on for a year or more? Are there questions to which you do not know the answer? Curiosity and the ability to constantly ask questions are useful qualities in finding and developing a research topic. Furthermore, the reader of your research is unlikely to find your thesis appealing if you, the author, do not find the topic interesting.

Problems, issues or conflicts

One possible strategy to find a research topic is to focus on specific problems, issues or conflicts that evoke your curiosity. By taking a look at different topics that dominate debates within the sciences, you will often find that good science has been inspired by social events (see section 7.2). One example is the scholarly interest during the 1940s and 1950s as to why some people became Nazis during the Second World War. Biologists, sociologists, political scientists, psychologists and historians conducted several studies to address this question from different perspectives. Another example is the interest in religious extremism and violence among political scientists, sociologists, historians and scholars of religion that appeared after the attacks on the World Trade Center in New York on September 11, 2001 and the bombings in London on July 7, 2005. It is also reasonable to believe that the terror attacks in Oslo on July 22, 2011 will result in new research. These examples show that science is closely related to the societies in which we live, which is also reflected in the topics chosen by scholars and students. An illustrative example is a master's thesis on electric car cultures. This student did an ethnographic study of the everyday use of electric vehicles in the UK (Brady, 2010). It would have been impossible to do this study only a few years ago. Many students find the topic for their thesis by taking a closer look at events, conflicts and problems in society.

Personal interests and experiences

Some students draw from *personal interest* during the process of finding a research topic. One example is a student with an interest in football. He used his master's thesis in social anthropology to study local Liverpool fans and their experiences of the commercial changes in the industry (Gustavsen, 2010). Another example is a student in North American studies who was interested in African American blues and hip hop. Her thesis explored the expression of dissent and social protest within these genres of music (Hansen, 2007).

It is also possible to begin by using your *personal experiences* to find and develop a research topic. One example is a student in social anthropology who grew up in an impoverished suburb of Buenos Aires, Argentina. She used her background and experiences with socioeconomic inequality to write a thesis that focused on the local responses to neo-liberal politics in a Uruguayan rural locality where a pulp mill had been installed (Salinas, 2010).

Not every personal experience is suitable for a research topic. If the topic becomes too personal and emotional, it might be difficult to create the necessary distance to write a good thesis. In some instances, fan studies, written by students who are fans of music, literature, film, football and other sports, tend to be implicit and positive, and often fail to ask difficult questions and raise critique of those who they admire. It is important to have a certain degree of distance so that perceptions are not clouded.

Profession or workplace

Some students find topics that are related to their own profession or workplace. Many students in nursing, social work and teaching write master's theses based on their work experiences. One example is a student who used to work as a secondary schoolteacher in London. She wrote a thesis on teaching methods developed for those working in caring professions (Nash, 2010). Another example is a student who conceived the idea for his thesis from his experiences both as a pupil and as a teacher in comprehensive schools in the north-east of England. His thesis focuses on pupil resistance to authority and its implications for pedagogic practices (Fortune, 2010). The advantages of this approach are that the student harbours knowledge of the field and has local access and trust. There are, however, some disadvantages to this approach as well. Students may lack critical distance and adopt the perspectives of the actors. They may also be tempted to consider colleagues and leaders to such an extent that scientific norms of truth and independence are sacrificed.

Research literature

Another way to find a topic is to take a closer look at the research literature. Is there a book or an article that impressed you? Does the literature discuss topics you find interesting? Is this something you will consider spending more time researching? Perhaps you think the author was limited in the way she or he addressed the topic? You should ask several types of questions to research literature (see section 6.3). Did the author leave out questions you think should be included? Or should the author have offered different interpretations?

A common strategy is to address gaps in current research (see section 8.2). Try to find phenomena that have received little or no attention by scholars. One student found that aspects of secular culture in Britain were neglected by sociological research. She used this gap as a reason to study the experiences of irreligion in individual lives (Lee, 2006).

Another strategy is to study the same phenomenon at different points in time. One example is a student in political science who analysed five American presidential elections between 1992 and 2008. By comparing different points in time, he explored the role that foreign policy issues played in these elections (Lian, 2010). A similar strategy is to study the same phenomenon in different contexts or in different key figures. For example, a student compared affirmative action in two different contexts, the US and the UK (Herron, 2010). Another example is a student who compared speeches delivered by two major politicians, Tony Blair and George W. Bush, during the same time period, from September 11, 2001 to the end of 2005 (Stenbakken, 2007). She was able to detect their different rhetorical styles by comparing their ideologies, rhetorical devices and modalities. Indeed, the use of comparisons, contrasts and differences are useful strategies when formulating research questions (see sections 7.1 and 7.2).

There are also different ways to use the literature to find a research topic. A common approach is to study two or more books or articles about a particular topic that interests you and to ask how they differ and why (see Chapter 7). Do they pose different questions? Do they use various types of data? Do they use alternative interpretations or modes of explanations? Do they define or use key concepts in different ways?

It is a good idea to study encyclopaedias, handbooks, companions and dictionaries to see if the review articles give you ideas (see section 5.7). At this early stage, skim reading is a must in order to avoid wasting time on topics you will not pursue. If you spend too much time studying the research literature before you have decided on a topic, you may risk becoming too dependent on the reading you have done. It is easy to be trapped into forming an opinion too readily on the basis of your reading. Many students overestimate the amount of knowledge needed to get started. Read some of the literature thoroughly and skim the rest. But read enough to be relatively well informed. You do not want to select a topic, only to discover that others have gone over the same ground before.

Classes and seminars

A good start in finding a topic is to make use of classes and seminars and talk with the professors (see section 4.3). Most of them are helpful in finding a topic. Some direct large research programmes and invite students to do a thesis within the frame of the programme. Others form research groups, where several students do their theses within the same or related fields.

Talk about it

Finally, it is helpful to discuss your ideas with other students. 'To talk about it' actually helps. Ask the other students about their topics and outline your own ideas (see section 4.2). Use social media and blogs by master's-level students to find more information about possible topics and discuss your ideas (see section 4.1). Later, use the social media and the blogs to present the findings from your study. When you have clarified your interests, paid attention to public debates, discussed with students and professors, studied literature and participated actively in class, you will find that these activities assist you in finding a research topic. This phase may take some time and it has its frustrations. Generally, students hope that good ideas will just appear out of the blue, but this is not how it works. Good ideas come when you search for new information and ask critical questions (see section 6.3).

1.2 Developing a topic

After you have found a topic that's caught your interest, it must be specified and developed further. The process of developing a topic will eventually lead to the formulation of research questions (see Chapter 7). During the early phase of this process, it is a good idea to work with several topics or several aspects of one topic. This will expand your ideas to include related topics. Eventually, you will find a topic you want to pursue. The aim here is to present a few useful techniques for developing topics.

Brainstorming

One method that will help you to find new ideas is brainstorming. This is a technique that will help you to *find* different ideas. Later, you go back and *evaluate* the suggestions you found. What you actually do is to sit down at your computer and write ideas without stopping. It does not matter whether you believe the ideas are good or bad, the issue for now is just to write them down. Before you start, make a decision to write, for example, for a period of five to ten minutes. When the time is over, go back and evaluate what you've written. Delete the ideas you do not like and keep the ones you believe can be developed further. With these new ideas in mind, repeat the process.

A common mistake among students is trying to be creative and judging new ideas simultaneously. You cannot come up with new ideas and label them as good or bad at the same time. This approach tends to limit creativity. Remember that finding ideas and evaluating them are two different processes. By letting yourself write down your ideas without stopping, and then going back and selecting the good from the bad, you are allowing yourself to be creative. This is the central structure in creative writing (see section 3.2).

Analogies

Another method for developing a topic is the use of analogies. Models that are proven to be useful in one field of study can sometimes be transferred to other fields. An example of the use of analogies is when theories about negotiations between political parties are applied to interpretations of negotiations between partners in the area of domestic work and childcare. Another example is when theories of decision making on the economic market are applied to other areas of decision making, such as participation in social movements. The method of using analogies requires familiarity with the literature in the field. You need theoretical knowledge to develop this application. Before you make serious efforts to use this method, ask your advisor if this is a good approach, otherwise, you may risk losing valuable time studying the wrong type of literature.

Mind map

Further, you can develop a topic by making a mind map. A mind map consists of mapping key concepts that are related to each other. In order to come up with ideas for relevant concepts, use the brainstorming method described above. You will find electronic tools for mind maps, brainstorming and planning for groups and individuals on Web 2.0 sites, and several are open source and free (e.g. see https://bubbl.us/). Some even provide opportunities for a group of students to share a mind map and work on it together to develop ideas. Let us say, for example, that the topic of your interest is 'social inequality' as shown in Figure 1.1.

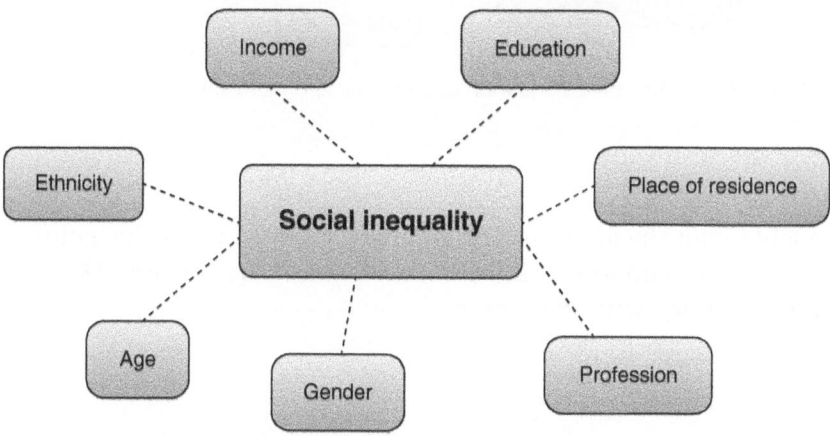

Figure 1.1 Initial mind map

This mind map gives you an *overview* of possible topics for a thesis (it is possible to add more ideas than shown). Develop the mind map further by selecting some concepts you think are related, and *group them* (see section 7.1). This group of ideas will, perhaps, create a conceptual starting point for a thesis. Draw arrows between the concepts you think constitute causal relationships. When you have completed your groupings, find one key concept and then repeat the process.

In our example, we have selected the concepts of income, education, ethnicity, age, gender and profession. These concepts can be the beginning of a study of educational performance among high-school students, as shown in Figure 1.2.

The method of drawing mind maps, as demonstrated in Figures 1.1 and 1.2, will help you to choose topics that can be developed further. By selecting some concepts and omitting others, you are specifying your research topic (see section 7.4). You may not readily understand why one concept is more

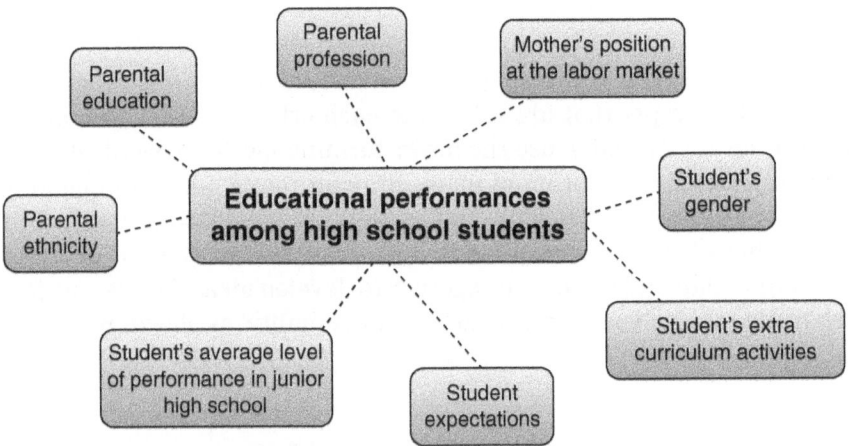

Figure 1.2 Concepts from initial mind map developed into a more specific study

developable than the other or why you have selected it. At this point, it is not important. The important issue is that you have begun. Defining your research questions will come later.

Asking open-ended questions

Finally, develop your topic by asking a few open-ended questions (see section 6.3). The different questions suggested below will, in some cases, indicate what type of methodological approach you will have to use in order to answer them (Barnes, 2005). These questions will vary somewhat within different fields of study:

- What is going on? (Surveys, evaluations, documentation, facts)
- Is this true? (Hypothesis testing, critique of sources)
- What happens if? (Trials, experiments, new methodology)
- What is the solution? (Problem solving)
- How can something be improved? (Evaluation, action research, applied research)
- Why is this happening? (Explanatory, analytical). (Barnes 2005: 108)

In some instances, a thesis will consist of one of these questions, and in other instances, a combination of two or more questions (see section 7.4). For example, if you want to answer the question 'What is going on?' you will search for documentation. To follow our example, we would like to map educational performance among high-school students. This might provide a basis for questions such as:

- 'Is this true?' (Is it true that children of well-educated parents get better grades than other students?)
- 'Why is this happening?' (Why do children of well-educated parents get better grades than other students?)
- 'What is the solution?' (What is needed to improve the grades of children whose parents have lower levels of education?)

Changes along the way

By developing your topic the way we have described here, changes will take place (see section 7.5). Perhaps you end up with a different topic than the one you initially found. Or perhaps you choose to focus upon issues you had not considered before. If you use this approach of specifying your topic several times, you will eventually develop a research topic.

Once you have an idea for a topic, be careful to avoid two common mistakes. One is selecting a topic that is too broad to be researchable: two examples are 'The role of the family in post-industrial society' or 'The significance of Islam in the Western world'. Be aware, though, that both topics can be developed further into research topics (see section 7). The other mistake is to select an 'overpopulated' topic: two examples are 'New analyses of the classical sociology of Max Weber' or 'The development and meaning of the concept "identity"'. There are topics within every field that have been researched to the extent that it is nearly impossible to present new and valuable information.

At this point, you should begin to consider if relevant data are available or if you must produce the data (Chapter 8). Ideally, a topic may be researchable even if it is impossible to collect relevant data. For example, it is theoretically possible to study the process of lobbying members of parliament, even if it is highly unlikely that you will collect a complete set of data.

When you have found one or more topics you would like to develop further, it is time to talk to your professor. She or he will help you to specify and develop your topics even further (see Chapter 4).

Finally, once you have selected a research topic and your professor agrees that it is viable, try to stick to your decision, unless you have good reasons to switch to another topic. It will help you avoid wasting time. It is difficult to write a thesis, and you will make it even more difficult for yourself if you change an agreed-upon topic (see section 7.5).

1.3 Research ethics

All research, including student research, is regulated by ethical norms and standards. Ethical concerns are relevant in several phases of your thesis. We will discuss these issues throughout the book. In the social sciences, several decisions are made which have an ethical dimension, including: the collection of data (section 8.3), writing (section 9.6), referencing different sources of information (section 11.4), and the student–advisor relationship (section 4.4).

Ethics during the research process and for the consequences of research

Research ethics relate to norms for behaviour during the research process and the responsibility of researchers for the consequences of their research (Hart, 2008a: 277–311). First and foremost you must have a fundamental respect for the people you are researching. Respect for people is relevant when you are deciding on a topic, during the research process and in communicating the research results.

When you are searching for a topic, consider the possible ethical issues involved. If you plan to use people as sources of information, you must know the laws and regulations that guarantee the right of privacy. The research process must demonstrate respect for individual liberty and autonomy, which means that you cannot begin data collection before you have the consent of the people involved. The research participants shall not be exposed for injuries or pain because they participate in your study. You must provide participants with all the necessary information to get a reasonable understanding of your project in order to give their informed consent to participation. They also have the right to withdraw their participation at any time without facing any form of negative consequences. Finally, you have an obligation to make the results of your research known by communicating them (e.g. by publishing them) in an understandable way.

Responsibility towards society

As a researcher, you also have a responsibility towards society, meaning that your study somehow should benefit society, either directly or indirectly. Based on the premise that research implies a search for new and better knowledge, research should not be affected by the interests of those who initiate the study. The funding institution should always be known to the public. As a master's student, you must adhere to the same ethical rules, regulations and reflections that established scholars do.

Ethics is not left to the individual. Therefore, several professional organizations have outlined formal codes of conduct so that all researchers, including students, can be aware of what is acceptable and what is unacceptable. Below are a few examples of ethical principles and codes of conduct for various groups of social scientists, as defined by some British and American organizations:

American Marketing Association: www.marketingpower.com/AboutAMA/Pages/Statement%20of%20Ethics.aspx

American Political Science Association: www.apsanet.org/pubs/ethics.cfm

Association of Social Anthropologists of the UK and the Commonwealth: www.theasa.org/ethics/Ethical_guidelines.pdf

The British Psychological society: www.bps.org.uk/what-we-do/ethics-standards/ethics-standards

The British Sociological Association: www.britsoc.co.uk/media/27107/StatementofEthicalPractice.pdf

Before you begin working on your thesis, get to know the ethical principles and codes of conduct that are relevant for you.

1.4 Writing a research proposal

Writing a research proposal is essential for all research. Often advisors and research committees require that you write a proposal for your work. If you want someone to fund your research, which is typically the case for any researcher, the research funding bodies require an excellent proposal in order to do so.

A research proposal is a plan for your work (for more information, see Hart, 2008a: 365–405). It is a map that outlines what you want to do, why you want to do it, how you want to do it, what you expect to find, and a plan that shows your ability to deliver what you promise. Remember to discuss your proposal with other students and, most importantly, with your advisor (see section 4). Your advisor knows what a research proposal should look like and will be able to guide you. If you have never written a proposal before, try to get the advice of someone who has been successful and ask if you can see a copy of their proposal. Also look at the Economic and Social Research Council's website (see www.esrc.ac.uk), which gives advice on 'How to write a good research proposal'. All of this will help you to understand what you are about to do, and save you time and effort.

Your research proposal will be a guide for your work, based on your design for your thesis (Chapter 8). This research design is related to the definition of your topic and your research questions (Chapters 1 and 7), a search and tentative description of the research literature (Chapters 5 and 6), your research methods (Chapter 8), plan for the analysis (Chapter 9), and ethical issues (sections 1.3, 8.3, 9.6 and 11.4).

You may ask why we discuss writing a research proposal here and not later in the book. It takes time to prepare and draft a research proposal because you will have to consider all aspects of the thesis. First, you need to know what the requirements for such a proposal are at your university. Then, you need to know something about a possible topic, the research literature, research methodology, research ethics and analysis before you begin your proposal. In order to find information that might help you, you can use this book actively by going back and forth. Finally, as you begin to work on your proposal, drafting and editing several times, you will begin to develop an outline of the work that lies ahead. This will help you in the planning process. There is also a certain excitement in anticipating what you might find and envisioning your work, accomplishment and future success (see Chapter 2). As you see, there are several reasons why it is a good idea to start the process of writing a research proposal early.

The main elements of a typical research proposal are outlined below. We have included references to where you will find relevant information in this book. In many ways, the structure of a research proposal is similar to a classic thesis structure (see section 11.1). One important difference is the *length of the research proposal*. The question of how long it should be depends on the requirements of your university, so do check this. A typical research proposal varies between 6 to 20 pages, which means that you have very little space to explain what you are going to do. While keeping spatial limits in mind, do not worry if your first drafts are too long; you will go back later and edit several times before you submit your proposal (see section 3.4 and Chapter 11).

- *Title and author:* Give a short title with a more specified subtitle. The title should describe what your research is about using as few words as possible. The title can be a working title, which you might want to change later; be aware that a change of title may have to be approved by your advisor or research committee.
- *Introduction:* A brief presentation of the thesis topic. Give a broad presentation of the theme and the narrative you are going to tell in the thesis. What is known about this topic, what you want to find out, and what are you going to do? How is your thesis different from that which is already known (see section 10.1)?
- *Aims and objectives:* What is the purpose of your research? Is there a particular problem in society that needs more knowledge, so your aim is to fill gaps in current research? Or do you think that previous research is mistaken and you want to propose an alternative approach? Perhaps you operate with a combination of several aims and objectives (see section 8.2).
- *Topic justification:* Why does this matter? Explain why this study is important. Will your work only have theoretical significance or will it have some sort of practical significance, such as to bring about some form of change (see section 7.3)?

- *Scope and limitations*: Due to very real limitations concerning time and money, you have to define the scope your research. Specify clearly the limitations of your thesis regarding theme, sample, geographical location and timeframe (see sections 7 and 8.2).
- *Literature review*: Give a brief overview of the relevant research literature. Search the literature and give an outline of the current research in the area, key concepts and debates (see section 5). What are the major issues and who represent the different positions? State the names of authors and their publications. How does the literature provide a frame for your thesis (see section 6)? Many students tend to give lengthy outlines of the research literature, and only add a few sentences when it comes to methods and practical issues regarding data collection. Unless you are writing a thesis where theory is the main issue, this is usually a mistake. The overview here is only meant to frame your thesis within current research.
- *Research questions*: Give a more detailed presentation of your overall research questions and all the specified questions your thesis will attempt to answer (see section 7).
- *Methods:* Present the methods you are going to use and the reasons for using them, based on the research questions. If you are going to use surveys or study specific groups of people or organizations, give detailed information about access. Have you gained permission to use the survey? Have people agreed to talk with you? It is time consuming to find out if you will be able to access the data you need, but this information is crucial. The more specific and realistic information you provide here, the more likely your advisor will think that you have the ability to conduct your thesis within your given timeframe.
- *Ethical considerations*: Include brief statements on how you intend to conform to ethical guidelines, and give detailed information about the different types of ethical issues and dilemmas you will need to deal with in your research (see sections 1.3 and 8.3).
- *Analytical approach*: Present briefly an outline of how you will analyse your data. If you write a quantitative study, somewhat detailed descriptions of the data and the statistical methods of analysis are required. Qualitative studies also require an outline of analytical approach (e.g. content, discourse, category, etc.) (see section 9).
- *Schedule*: Include a timetable for your work where you estimate the time it will take to complete your thesis. The timetable should be a realistic estimate of the time the work will take you (see section 1.5 and the summary below).
- *References*: Provide an alphabetical list of references that occur in the proposal (see section 11.7).

1.5 Project planning

As soon as you get started, make a plan for your work. Perhaps you will object and say that making a plan is a waste of time because you will never stick to it anyway. The purpose of a plan is not necessarily to stick to it for the sake of doing it: the purpose is to give you an overview and help you structure the work you are about to take on.

When you start making your plan, write a detailed list of all the things you need to do to finish your thesis. Include everything you remember, from finding a research topic to reviewing the research literature and contacting people. Then, structure your list according to deadlines. What do you need to do first, and what can wait? Organize the various tasks according to each semester you plan to use on your thesis. What are the things that need to be done each semester? Organize the first semester month by month. When the first semester is over, make a monthly plan for the next semester. You might find that you spend more time than you planned to do, but this is not a valid reason for avoiding to plan the next semester. During the last few months and weeks before you submit the thesis, careful planning is a must (see section 12).

It is a good idea to go over your plans at the end of every month. What did you do and what remains to be done? If you did not accomplish all the things you planned, what were the reasons? Did you make unrealistic deadlines for yourself? Did some of the work take more time than you thought? Or were there other factors outside your control that delayed your work? Equally important, are there areas where you spent too much time? Your original plan will be adjusted on a regular basis. Some things will, perhaps, be moved. Others will be taken out, and some new things will be added. By setting deadlines for your work, you put pressure on yourself to finish. You may need this pressure, especially when you are going through a difficult phase.

1.6 Summary

1. Remember that this phase offers a number of frustrations, as well as new discoveries.
2. You need to find a research topic. You can search several places:
   - your own interests
   - problems, issues or conflicts in society
   - personal experiences and interests
   - profession or workplace
   - previous research
   - classes and seminars
   - talk with other students and use social media
   - talk with your professor, so that you know that the topic you select is a good research topic – she or he has the skills, abilities and professional mandate to help you see whether a topic has the potential to be developed into a research topic.
3. Once you have found a topic, it must be specified and developed further. Use the following techniques to develop a topic:

- brainstorming
- analogies
- mind-mapping
- asking open-ended questions.

4 All research is regulated by ethical norms and standards. Ethics is not left to the individual, but there are formal codes of ethics for social science researchers and students. It is your responsibility to get to know them. These are some of the ethical norms that should guide your research:

- the people involved must give their consent
- the participants must receive all the necessary information about your project to give their consent
- the participants shall not be exposed to injuries or pain because they participate
- people have the right to withdraw their participation at any time
- you must make the results of your research known
- it is your responsibility that your research should somehow be of benefit to society.

Remember that the student–advisor relationship is also guided by ethical codes and standards.

5 Begin your work with the research proposal early, as this is time consuming. A research proposal is a very brief map for your work, which includes:

- title and author name
- introduction
- aims and objectives
- topic justification
- scope and limitations
- literature review
- research questions
- methods
- ethical considerations
- analytical approach
- schedule
- references

6 As soon as you get started, make a plan for your work. The Gantt chart is a standard form for project work. It is used to give an overview of the time schedule and all the activities involved. Several different computer programs can be used to draw these charts electronically, where some are open source and free and some must be purchased. It is possible to make a simple chart in Microsoft Word, which we have done in Figure 1.3.

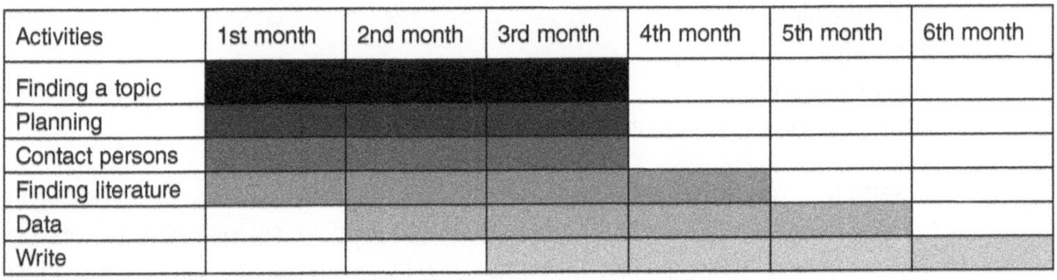

Activities	1st month	2nd month	3rd month	4th month	5th month	6th month
Finding a topic						
Planning						
Contact persons						
Finding literature						
Data						
Write						

Figure 1.3 Gantt chart for the first semester of doing a master's thesis

1.7 Action plan

1. Select two or three topics that interest you. Develop them by using an electronic mind map:
   - Fill in a key concept taken from one of the topics.
   - Fill in related concepts.
   - Select some concepts and group them.
   - If you think there are causal relationships between some concepts, draw arrows between them.
   - Repeat the process.

2. Select one of the topics you were working with above:
   - Ask all the questions listed on pages 8–9.
   - Which questions do you find relevant?
   - Which combinations of questions are useful?

3. Plan your thesis by drawing a Gantt chart where you fill out all the activities for the thesis in the left column. Make different charts on the basis of a year, semester and month.

4. Go over the charts at the end of every period:
   - What did you accomplish?
   - What remains to be done?
   - If you were unsuccessful in sticking to your plan, why was this so?
   - What can you improve?

2
Overcoming barriers and getting started

Some students struggle with the writing process and have difficulties getting started. Other students think that the writing itself goes fairly well, but they are unable to manage time and have few routines for the writing process. We would like to address some aspects of the psychology of writing that we think are relevant for many master's-level students. Our hope is that this chapter will help you to identify and overcome barriers that prevent you from writing.

It is generally taken for granted that every graduate student has good writing skills. However, many advisors know that this is far from the truth. Like any other skill, the ability to write varies from person to person. There are several reasons for this. One explanation lies in the educational methods and priorities when you first learned how to write: if the essential skills were spelling and grammar, and you had little choice in selecting topics for your writing projects, you may feel that writing is mechanical and has little connection with your own thoughts. Other explanations are related to individuals. The joys and sorrows of your own past experiences with writing influence your current emotions and behaviour. Further, individual motivation, regular practice and habits all impact on the development of your writing skills. These are factors you can control and change. We believe that every graduate student can become a competent writer in spite of inadequate teachers, underdeveloped skills and poor habits. This is, of course, dependent upon personal commitment to work towards desired improvement.

When you are going to write a master's thesis, you must learn the required style for this genre. We all know that a good poet does not necessarily make a good novelist, or that a good novelist does not necessarily make a good scientist. The reason is that each genre has its own style. Whether it is an essay or a term paper, you must be familiar with the genre in question. When you are going to write a master's thesis, learn the scientific genre with its requirements concerning writing style, composition and argumentation.

It is impossible in a book like this to deal with every personal aspect of writing (for more information, see Rudestam and Newton, 2007). Here we will outline some of the most common challenges facing students who want to improve their writing and how to handle them. The overview is meant as a guidance that points to issues that need further study and work. Our hope is that the information will assist you in overcoming barriers, accessing coping skills and growing as a writer.

2.1 Writing blocks

Many advisors experience that students need more help than technical supervision and consultation to complete their thesis. Writing a thesis for the first time seems to trigger emotional issues and create blows to self-esteem. In addition to the common questions and doubts of topic or method, many students feel frustrated when doing an independent work of this size, and the task at hand can seem overwhelming. Some experience writing blocks as soon as they start work. Writing blocks haunt the best of writers, sometimes for extended periods. However, most writers develop strategies they employ to make sure they continue to write.

Emotional and cognitive blocks

Writing blocks can be emotional, cognitive or behavioural, or a combination. When beginning to work on a thesis, students often have to face deeply felt beliefs about their own incompetence. They think that they are not as intellectually capable as other students and unable to complete such a task. Some think that they do not deserve a good grade or that the thesis will never be completed or accepted. Often such beliefs stand in the way of progress of the thesis. By exploring these feelings and talking with others about them, many students find that they can identify coping skills and make use of them to overcome their own barriers.

Another source of writing blocks can stem from previous writing experiences. When the authors of this book were children, spelling, grammar and penmanship were highly valued qualities, and we often had to write on topics selected by the teachers. Contemporary students have experienced more emphasis on creative writing and freedom in selecting topics. Based on previous experiences with writing, many people have learned to distance themselves from writing. They feel that writing is not an activity that is related to issues they feel strongly about. By selecting a topic of interest, many students discover that they can use writing to give themselves a voice on important issues.

Some people have also learned that writing is boring. Boredom is a state of mind usually related to a disconnection with the topic or a lack of interest. If writing seems boring, the chances are you have selected a topic that does not interest you. Boredom is also a common result if you feel that writing implies expressing someone else's thoughts. Do not fall victim to the excuse that you are bored because you have a difficult task at hand. This may become a self-imposed barrier. Try to look at writing as a tool to develop and express your own ideas.

Others have developed low self-esteem when it comes to writing. It is difficult to get started if previous responses to your written work have been along the lines of: 'You write very poorly. You do not know the first thing about grammar. You must throw it away and start over.' Any pleasures in writing that the student may have felt initially are diluted, and many students end up being afraid of writing. Further below we will discuss in more detail strategies that you can use to overcome these obstacles. A vague response like 'This looks OK' also creates problems. The student is often left with a number of questions: 'Was my work good or bad? Did the advisor actually read it? Was the advisor trying to be nice? What should I do to improve the text?' Demand clarity from your advisor. Ask questions and expect answers that will help you to develop your skills.

Task blocks

Some forms of writing blocks stem from behaviour. They are not related to emotional issues or past experiences, but are connected to tasks that must be done. Many students do not know what to write because they lack the necessary knowledge to do so. If you do not know much about a topic, you have little to say. The problem is that you have not acquired the prerequisites for writing. The ability to write academic texts requires some preliminary work. If you do not write because you have gaps in your knowledge, read about the topic and do your research.

Many students do not write because they have developed poor habits. Some decide to write when they are inspired, which means that they constantly postpone it. They do not write regularly, but only when they have a deadline to meet. They do not have a specific place where they write, but they write a little bit here and there, often in places where they are disturbed by noise.

It takes time to change behavioural patterns. This is especially true when the patterns are based on previous negative experiences. Established writers have learned to deal with these issues and they have developed techniques to handle pressures and negative critique. For the less experienced writer, such as the graduate student, these problems can exacerbate their self-doubts and they will struggle to keep writing. Therefore, we will discuss these issues in more detail.

2.2 Processing information and making decisions

In this section, we will attempt to explain how some emotional and cognitive writing blocks are formed. We will do so by outlining how you process new information, react to it and make decisions. Many tasks you do in relation to the thesis are based on your decision-making skills. For this reason, it is important to know about positive and negative factors that might affect the decisions you make.

The issues discussed here can be applied to several areas of your life, not just writing. Our hope is that this information will help you to reach your goal and finish the thesis. More specifically, we will examine the effects of negative response and critique upon your self-image, and how this affects your decision making (Bolton, 1986).

Decision making

Some decisions appear to require little or no thought. You make them without having to think. They are learned behaviour patterns or habits. For example, you may have a number of writing habits you have never considered. Other

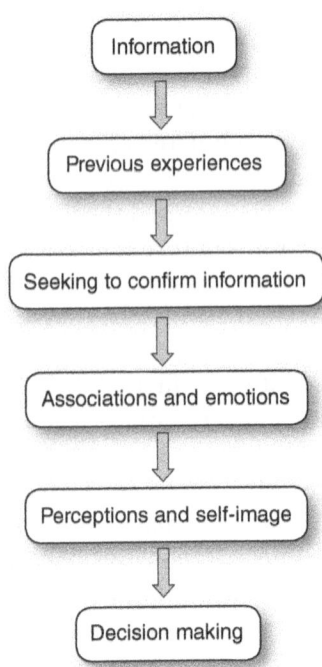

Figure 2.1 Model for decision making

decisions require conscious reflections. When you sign up for a class or apply for a job, you carefully assess benefits and costs. If you decide to improve your writing skills, this decision will hopefully be the result of careful reflections (see Figure 2.1).

Previous experiences and confirming information

Let us imagine that you received a response to your writing along the lines we mentioned above. We are not talking about constructive critique that outlines how to improve your writing, but negative and limiting statements such as 'You cannot write!'. If this is the response you get, you will ask yourself 'Have I heard or experienced this before?'. You will seek to confirm the information with previous experiences. If you have heard similar statements before, you may be receptive to believing the negative statements you are now hearing.

Associations, emotions and self-image

Critique is expressed in words. Words cue associations and emotions that are rooted in previous experiences. Emotions will often manifest themselves as embarrassment and frustration. They will have a tendency to affect your attitude, which is important when you are going to make decisions about further actions. If the images and emotions are pleasant, you will have a positive attitude. If they are negative, they are often followed by negative self-talk: 'They are right. I always make mistakes. I am not a good writer. I never was.' This form of self-talk will reinforce your self-image in a negative direction. As a result, your tendency will be to question your ability to write.

2.3 The motivation to write

So far, we have discussed how negative patterning can result in de-motivation and impair attempts to improve your writing skills. Here, we will point out alternative ways to react and function, given the same point of departure. You must decide what it is you want. Then you must determine what is necessary to achieve these goals. Do you want to get a good grade on your thesis? Have you seriously considered a PhD? Do you want to be a respected writer? If so, understand that this is possible if you analyse your behavioural patterns, modify your habits and make a conscious decision to improve your writing. This demands commitment and time.

Re-evaluate your self-image

Belief systems about who we are as people can be empowering or limiting. When did you first decide to go to university? Was it expected in your family? Belief systems colour your self-image and affect your expectations about your own achievements. Which professional goals can you see in the future? Which limitations do you have for how far you can go? Upon what premise have you taken this position? Is it because of a lack of skills or uncertainty in your abilities? Ask yourself: Have others ever been wrong about what is possible for you? Have you been wrong in underestimating your skills and abilities? If the answer is 'yes', focus on achieving more control over your life. Could you achieve more, if you take full accountability for what you think is personally attainable?

One effective method to affect the self-image is to confirm who you are through self-talk: 'This is me. I can learn to become a good writer. I can see myself submitting a master's thesis.' Every time you make such a statement, you are affirming who you are and who you want to become. Change does not come overnight, but this method helps you to adjust and therefore affects your self-image. This sounds simple, but in the final analysis it actually is more important who you want to become rather than who you are today.

Visualization

Another method to impact change is visualization. It is possible to simulate positive experiences. By visualizing an experience and its positive outcome, you will positively impact your belief system. Visualization can help you to change your self-image and rid yourself of the fears that keep you from trying (Brennan, 1990: 93–94). Think of your first time behind the wheel learning to drive. You had to believe it was possible for you to learn it. You needed to trust the driving instructor (sometimes we all need heroes, experts and wizards). Next, you placed the visual image of yourself, the perfect driver, in your mind. If your instructor was a positive person who encouraged you, you tried again and again, no matter what the outcome was of the first attempts. Small successful steps are the key, and becoming a little better is crucial. Did you learn how to drive? The nucleus for change and growth is desire. Often the only thing standing in the way of what you want to achieve is yourself. By working to remove your own barriers, you will help yourself to increase your level of achievement.

Success and failure

It is important to have success. Sometimes, it is equally important to fail. Why? Because failure teaches you new wisdom and takes you in a different direction. When confronted with failure or a negative result, you must analyse the situation and structure a plan to redirect your efforts. Perhaps this means that you need to get help. After you have grappled with the problem and sought help, it is time to put it away for some time. This is called *creative distancing*. When you acquiesce, you may find that the solution comes to you as if from out of the blue. Successful students are successful in spite of failures and difficulties. This is not necessarily due to intellect (even if this helps), but primarily as a result of beliefs, redirected efforts and perseverance.

2.4 Getting started

Even if many students struggle with some of the issues we mentioned above, most find that regular writing is extremely important. Indeed, good routines are prerequisites for developing writing skills. All skills require regular practice and most of us impose discipline in our lives and set aside time to do the things that are important to us. We describe below some strategies that you can use to get started and develop routines for writing.

Space

Arrange a space that is set aside for writing and studying. It does not need to be a separate room; it can be a desk in the corner of your bedroom or living room. What you need is privacy and a place that is free from distractions. Make this place sacrosanct, so that you associate it with writing and studying. Once you sit down, your mind will turn to the writing process. Talk with the people in your life to respect the time you are working at your desk.

Schedule

Establish a regular weekly schedule that allows for several hours of concentrated time to work on your thesis. Some students work well early in the morning. Others like to write late in the evening. Some prefer reserving a few hours every day, whereas others like to work two or more full days. Whatever you prefer, you need to know your best work time. Your schedule will also be affected by other commitments in your life. The important issue is to reserve regular blocks of thesis time. A firm schedule will help you when you do not feel like writing or when obstacles arise. If writing at regular hours is new to you, perhaps you should begin with 1–2 hours per day for 3–4 days a week. It is important to take your work as a student seriously enough to organize your life so that your writing time is as important as the time you reserve for other activities. If you want to improve your writing and get the thesis finished, it is essential to make writing a regular activity.

Divide the tasks into manageable pieces

Considering the thesis as a whole, it can seem fairly overwhelming. Deal with the thesis one step at a time by dividing the tasks into manageable pieces. A good place to begin is to make a list of all the things you need to do, from finding a topic to reviewing the literature and researching the data situation (see section 1.5 about project planning). By prioritizing the things on your list you are structuring your writing project, which will help to get you started.

Formulate thoughts into sentences

Get your thoughts formulated into written sentences. If you write only one paragraph, you have started. A good idea is to focus on finding a topic for your thesis and developing it. We have already mentioned *brainstorming* and *mind maps* as methods to find and develop ideas (section 1.2). Later, we will suggest more tricks to keep you writing (see section 3.4).

Assess your writing skills

Make an assessment of your writing skills and become aware of your strengths and weaknesses (see section 2.6). Usually, a student will master one area better than another. Some have problems with spelling, whereas others find it difficult to formulate complete sentences or compose a coherent text. Some students feel that it is difficult to argue a point, and there are those who tend to voice their views without any documentation to support them. By assessing your writing skills, you will identify your challenges and know what to work on and develop.

Prioritize the thesis

Completing a master's thesis is demanding and needs priority. This means that other activities in life will be put on hold for a period of time. One reason for delays and why some students never finish the thesis is because they fall prey to distractions. If you have the ability to prioritize your time and target your efforts, you will increase the likelihood of completing your thesis.

Prioritize your personal life

It is also important to prioritize your personal life when writing a thesis. Many graduate-level students have significant others in their lives, and it is important to be sensitive to their needs. Find out how to balance their needs together with the pursuit of your degree. Talk with them and negotiate about ordinary responsibilities and time. A partner who is not understanding or flexible can become a hindrance to progress. However, most students find that they receive love and support from their families and friends during this period.

2.5 Summary

1. Emotional and cognitive writing blocks can be related to:
   - beliefs about your own incompetence
   - previous experiences with writing
   - perceptions of writing as boring
   - low self-esteem when it comes to writing.

2. Some writing blocks stem from behaviour, such as:
   - little knowledge of the topic
   - poor writing routines and habits.

3. Decisions are often made based on:
   - information
   - previous experiences
   - confirmations of information
   - associations, emotions and self-image.

4. Methods you can use to motivate yourself to write:
   - re-evaluate your self-image
   - visualize the desired experience and positive outcome
   - use failure to redirect your efforts.

2.6 Action plan

1. Make an overview of your current writing routines. Then, make a detailed list of new writing routines for this semester:
   - arrange a space where you can write in privacy
   - schedule blocks of time for writing by specifying days and hours.

- make it a priority and determine to follow through with the new routines outlined above
- discuss your schedule with the people in your life; this will help to win the support you need when working on your thesis.

2 Make an assessment of your writing skills. Which writing skills are good, and which writing skills do you need to develop?

- grammar, spelling
- writing complete sentences and a coherent text
- developing ideas
- developing arguments
- basing your viewpoints on facts and research.

3

Basic rules of writing

A common starting point for every writer is to know the basic rules and methods for writing. Further, it is helpful to know about different styles of writing. Think of the styles of writing as tools you employ to reach your target audience. By becoming familiar with the toolbox you will know how the different tools function. We will, further, outline how to create structure in your writing and use paragraphs to construct an overall argumentation. Finally, we will provide a practical guide to help you begin writing, and to keep writing on days when it gets difficult.

3.1 Some rules for good writing

There are some simple, basic rules of writing that must be accepted in order to write well. These are the same for the beginning writer as for the accomplished writer. Here we will focus upon three rules that are related to the target audience, distance to the subject matter and the purpose of your writing.

The audience

The first rule is to do with defining the target audience. Writing is a form of communication that involves the writer as well as the potential reader. No matter what you write, it is important to write with an awareness of who the readers are so that you can imagine what they need to know to understand your ideas. Will your writing be addressing the general public, other graduate students or the faculty on the thesis committee? What are the professional and the educational make-up of the potential readers? Asking these types of questions will enable you to imagine their needs and interpretive skills. This determines the acceptable style of writing so that you communicate your ideas in the clearest possible way. When you are writing a master's thesis, your target audience is the thesis committee, which consists of faculty within your field. You will be evaluated by someone who is well educated and has an interest in your topic, but who does not necessarily have detailed knowledge of it. Indeed, many types of writing are directed at the uninformed but interested reader. Additionally, you will want to show the members on your committee that you have acquired the craftsmanship of doing a scientific piece of work.

Since the target audience is the thesis committee, some students fail to explain important concepts or demonstrate their understanding of the overall argument. Instead, they believe that a mere reference to them is sufficient. This form of writing is too implicit. It is better to explain a concept and an argument too much than too little. Also, some students explain concepts by referring to formal definitions. A more fruitful approach is to demonstrate your understanding of concepts by explaining them in the text.

Any good writer demonstrates respect for the audience. Do not write above the level of your potential readers, and at the same time do not underestimate their intelligence. When writing a master's thesis, show the professors that you have a broad orientation, which is evident in the discussion of respected research. In order to be taken seriously, support your statements with research and avoid undocumented personal opinions.

Personal investment

This takes us to the second rule. Be aware of your personal investment in the topic. As mentioned before, choosing a topic that interests you can facilitate your writing. Being passionate about a topic can give you energy and creativity. This may be a passionate desire to find answers to specific questions, or a passionate curiosity about certain issues or a passion to communicate to the reader important information you have found through your research. Your investment in the topic will often make your writing interesting to others, and it can help you to develop your 'writing voice' (Rudestam and Newton, 2007: 238–242). Sometimes you will find that your interest in a topic increases as you learn more about it; this can become an asset when developing your argument. What were your initial beliefs and ideas pertaining to the topic? How did your reading and research develop your ideas? A topic that engages you will also create motivation and determination during difficult periods.

However, choosing topics with high personal investment can impair your judgement and approach. Are you using the thesis to support your established views and notions? Sometimes passion about a topic can make you lean too much to one side or the other without having enough documentation to support it. An awareness of your personal investment can help you spot your own biases. Are you willing to interact with the material and test the ideas and information found in the research literature against your own thoughts? Are you open to the possibility that your research can prove you wrong? Or is the topic so personal that it is difficult to approach it with a certain degree of objectivity? These are some of the questions you should consider, because scholarly writing and research requires the author to go beyond personal passion to reach conclusions based on collected material. Good authors combine personal passion with collected information and integrate the two, while being open that the research process can prove them wrong.

Conventional scholarly writing used to refer to the self as 'we' or a third person and never as 'I', in order to create distance and a sense of objectivity. One example is 'We find in our data that …' when, in fact, the author is a single person who collected and analysed the data. Today, this convention is outdated and most academics think that using 'we' in this sense sounds pretentious and pompous. If you are the person who collected and analysed the data, it is more accurate to state 'I found in my data …'. The word 'we' is used when referring to a co-authored text, like this book, or when referring to a group of people like 'the general public' or 'social scientists'. It is also used when the author wants to include the reader, for example: 'In this chapter, we have seen that …'. Referring to the author as a third person is still common in scholarly writing. In the example above, this would be something like 'The data show that …'. This form keeps a focus on the issue and distances the author from personal engagement. If you prefer to use 'I', be consistent but do not overuse it. It can give the impression of an author who is too engaged in the subject matter, so that the text seems like a personal confession rather than an academic-style text. Trying to find the right style can be difficult. It is a good idea to create some variety by using different phrases, such as: 'There is disagreement between …' and 'This view was opposed by …'. Study the text of other authors to find alternative phrases.

The purpose of writing

The third rule relates to awareness of the purpose of the work. Why are you putting your fingers to the keyboard? Do you write for your own benefit, or do you hope that it will benefit others in society? In some instances, the purpose of writing is to work through thoughts and ideas you are grappling with. In other instances, the purpose is to enlighten your fellow human beings about issues that concern you. Most master's students, however, write with the purpose of finishing their thesis so that they can graduate.

The purpose of your writing will determine your style, structure and method. There are completely different rules of writing to a chronicle in a newspaper than to notes in a diary when it comes to level of knowledge, argument and linguistic skills. Likewise, there are specific requirements in a master's thesis as it relates to linguistic precision, critical sense, use of scientific methods and well-documented argumentation. In order for you to reach your goal of finishing the thesis and graduating, it is essential that you learn the requirements and skills needed to write a thesis. It is a good idea to read completed master's theses, which you will find at the university library in paper or electronic format.

3.2 Writing styles

Based on the audience for your writing, we will distinguish between three forms of writing styles: persuasive writing, compulsory writing and uninvited writing (Elbow, 1981: 200–215).

Persuasive writing

The persuasive form can take the shape of an essay, a master's thesis or a piece in the newspaper. Persuasive writing is built upon the pillars of a strong central argument (Elbow, 1981: 201). First, you present good arguments for the position you hold. Thereafter, you put effort into finding arguments that are contrary to yours, which you attempt to refute. If your goal is to persuade the reader, this is a good strategy (for more information on critical analysis, see section 6.4). The strength in your argumentation lies in your ability to refute the opponent's arguments.

The aim of a persuasive piece is not to convince the reader, but simply to present the possibility that you are right. If a writer gets the audience to accept the possibility that an explanation can be true or that the writer might be correct, the writer has done her or his job. Likewise, if the audience can be directed to question their ideas and ask if there is another way of looking at the same facts, nothing more needs be accomplished. From this point on, the readers will be examining their ideas and attempting to validate or refute them. A presentation of mere facts makes for boring reading. The form in persuasive writing must be simple: present your arguments clearly and leave complex sentence structures aside. Contrast the pro and counter arguments and help the reader to consider the possibility that you may be correct.

Compulsory writing

The best example of compulsive writing is the master's thesis. This writing is designed to demonstrate acquired knowledge, critical thought and reflection, and the ability to conduct a scientific project. Since the purpose of this form of writing is to pass the exam, you must adhere to a few requirements and rules set by the institution where you are a student.

Uninvited writing

Uninvited writing is deemed by most students to be the most fun form of writing. It is creative and innovative. It is labelled 'uninvited' because it is thought to begin without a target audience. This has proven to be a misconception, as the writer often has an audience in mind, whether this is the general public or yourself. When you want to practise writing, use the uninvited writing style to write about anything you want.

3.3 Structure

Here we will see how you structure sentences and paragraphs (Barrass, 2002: 30–53). If you do not have structure it is very difficult to express a point of view or construct a logical argument.

The sentence

The sentence must have a subject and a verb. It can also have descriptive modifiers in the form of adjectives and adverbs. Try to place *subject and verb early in the sentence*, as the text becomes easier to read. This is an example of a complicated sentence: 'Based on a survey of a representative sample of women above 50, a study was conducted of their smoking habits.' The message that a study has been conducted comes towards the end of the sentence, therefore this sentence should be reformulated. How?

The sentences must *be grammatically correct*. This means that you must keep to the same *tense of the verb* within the same sentence, and often within the same paragraph. For example, 'The lectures were conducted, and the students have received information about the lesson plan' should be changed to either 'The lectures *were* conducted, and the students *received* information about the lesson plan' or 'The lectures *have been conducted*, and the students *have received* information about the lesson plan'.

If you want to write well, you must learn how to use a precise style. Most issues can be said in simple words, and a complicated sentence can be simplified without losing its meaning. For example, 'Within the frames of the budget of the university, one does not have the possibility to conduct more hiring this year' can be simplified to 'The university cannot afford to hire more people'. Take a critical look at your sentences and try to reformulate them. If you truly understand your own writing, you will express yourself clearly. Also, it is easier to communicate complicated ideas when using a simplistic writing style.

Some sentences are so general that they are almost meaningless. Let us give you an example and ask what is wrong with the following statement: 'The students at the university are getting educated to unemployment.' Here are some of the questions that should be posed for the sentence to become meaningful:

- Which students are we talking about? Are they students at a particular university, or are we talking about all university students in a particular state or country?
- Is the statement true for all students, the majority or just a few?
- What type of unemployment are we talking about?

General sentences raise a number of questions and possibilities of interpretation. Your language should be so precise that there is no doubt about what you mean. How can the above statement be reformulated and improved? What do you suggest?

The topic sentence – a means of structuring the paragraph

The topic sentence is usually the first in a paragraph. It describes what is to follow and is a contract with the reader. The topic sentence states what you will discuss in the paragraph. It might lead to a question you want to pose afterwards, but it should not be formulated as a question. The topic sentence contains *the controlling idea* in the paragraph. Once you have presented it, do not disappoint the reader by changing the topic. If you want to change the topic, it should be in the closing of the paragraph, as a conclusion or the beginning of a new paragraph.

The topic sentence usually consists of three parts: noun, verb and a controlling idea (Gallo and Rink, 1991: 3). The noun is, of course, what the sentence is about, and the verb gives information about the noun. The controlling idea usually follows these main parts and describes the noun in one way or another. For example:

> J.K. Rowling is a well-read author. Her books about Harry Potter have sold more than 400 million copies and been adapted into several films.

It is easy to see that the noun in this topic sentence is the author with the pseudonym J.K. Rowling. One aspect of her is selected that will be developed further in the paragraph. The topic sentence limits a larger topic and describes only aspects of the noun with a controlling idea. The function of the controlling idea is to focus on certain aspects of the noun and excludes other aspects. When the topic sentence is going to be developed into a paragraph, some information or documentation must be offered to support the proposition expressed in the controlling idea. The topic sentence must therefore be concise and followed by indicators that will either support or weaken the controlling idea.

Take a look at the following sentence and use the criteria mentioned above to decide if the sentence lends itself to paragraph development:

> Helen is an intelligent and capable student.

This sentence describes a noun with two adjectives: intelligence and capability. In order to fulfil the contract with the reader, the writer must offer proof statements of Helen's intellect and capability. It might include Helen's grades, scholarship or her publications.

An important feature of a topic sentence is that it is formulated in a way that it can be developed further. By 'developed', we mean that more information can be added about the controlling idea. The controlling idea must be interesting as well. It is the hook you use to keep the interest of the reader. By learning to write good topic sentences, structuring and writing a paragraph will be that much easier.

The paragraph

Constructing paragraphs can be exciting. This is because it is easy to learn in a relatively short time. In only five to six lines you can demonstrate your new writing skills. The first sentence indicates your ability to present an idea and formulate it into an engaging and provable topic sentence. Your understanding of the idea will be demonstrated in the second to third sentences. The logic and the ability to reason are seen in the next two sentences, because this is where propositions, contrasts and comparisons are placed. The paragraph is concluded with one to two sentences. Paragraphs usually have the following structure:

1 Topic sentence, inclusive a controlling idea.
2 Clarifying sentence.

3 Propositions:
    - supporting sentences
    - contrast and comparisons.
4 Concluding sentence stating findings and conclusions.

Not every element in the paragraph will have the same emphasis. Below we will take a look at the construction of a paragraph in a master's thesis. The topic of the thesis is the role of foreign policy in American presidential elections, and the student is discussing the 1996 election when Bill Clinton and Bob Dole were running for office (Lian, 2010). Notice how he presents the controlling idea in the topic sentence, followed by a brief elaboration of the topic:

> The 1996 election is something of a black hole in American elections studies, especially with respect to the role of foreign policy. The main reason … is the general impression that foreign policy played little to no role in the election as economic issues took the center stage once again (Alvarez and Nagler, 1998). (Lian, 2010: 28)

Next, he presents a proposition:

> Neither the mainstream media nor the candidates themselves focused on foreign policy and the differences between the candidates on these issues were perceived as limited (Bennett and White, 2002: 19–20). (ibid.: 28)

The proposition is supported and nuanced by documentation:

> Pomper (1997: 189) attributes the lack of foreign policy focus to 'the end of open international conflicts' after the Cold War. Wanniski (1999: 113–129) … states that this was not a result of a lack of critical foreign policy issues. According to him, the lack of foreign policy focus in the election originated from certain characteristics of the candidates. Bob Dole is described as an old-school conservative from rural Kansas who viewed the President as the undisputed commander-in-chief and that he should command public support regardless of what foreign policies he initiated. Clinton on the other hand came into the White House in 1993 directly from the position of governor in Arkansas and had at the time little or no distinct views when it came to foreign policy. He therefore let more experienced Democrats greatly influence the formation of foreign policy in his first period. These Democrats had been quite tightly knit to their Republican counterparts in the last part of the Cold War through the House and Senate committees on foreign relations and the Council of Foreign Relations (Wanniski 1999: 113–114). (ibid.: 28)

The last sentence functions as a summary and conclusion to the paragraph:

> Because of this intriguing connection, Clinton's positions on foreign policy were situated quite close to the positions of the Republican establishment. (ibid.: 28)

Once you have begun writing, whether you are writing about the thesis topic or reviewing the research literature, this is a useful way to structure the material.

3.4 Tricks to continue writing

You have designated space for writing and scheduled a block of time, and now you are in front of the screen. Many students say that they feel empty in this situation. They have little to say. Or perhaps you wrote well yesterday, but do not know where to begin today. It is easy to postpone writing in these situations. Fortunately, below is some practical advice that should be helpful (see also section 2.4).

Write – anything!

If you do not write much, it is important that you practise writing. You should actually practise writing words and sentences, even if the topic is trivial. One way of getting started and to keep practising is to write a dairy. Or you may write something that you like, such as poetry or an issue that concerns you. Practise writing descriptions. This is a form of uninvited writing. Another form of practising is to write a summary with complete sentences based on notes taken during a lecture. Teach yourself to summarize a topic in a paragraph, as outlined above. Practice a minimum of 5–10 pages every week: poetry, short stories, blogs, or pieces to the newspaper. It is important that you write as precisely as you can, no matter the purpose of your writing. Even if you perhaps feel that this has little to do with your thesis, it will actually help you practise writing, which will be of benefit to the thesis later. The more you write, the better writer you will become.

Use the brainstorming method

If you have problems knowing what to write on a specific topic, one idea is to use the brainstorming method (see section 1.2). Choose an aspect of the topic and write all ideas relating to it that come to your mind. To get started, put your fingers on the keyboard and write continually for a limited period, say five minutes. When you are finished, read what you've written. Perhaps one or two sentences are useful. You can use these as a starting point and repeat the process.

Stop while you have good ideas

Some feel that the problem is not writing in and of itself, once they get started. The problem is this: starting again. Even if you wrote well yesterday, the problem is to know how to continue the next day. One advice is to stop writing while you still have good ideas. Write down your ideas in whole sentences, so that you will remember them the next day. You will not have to start your day with an empty mind. Instead, you can begin with yesterday's notes.

Begin early with reviewing the research literature

In order to start writing the thesis itself, a good place to begin is to review the research literature (see section 6.2). When you are going to review what other authors have written, you do not have to come up with and formulate new ideas. You only have to write a summary of something you have read. Begin with the introduction, because this is where you find the topics and the questions of the book or the article. Then concentrate on the conclusion, where you find the results and the conclusions. It is also a good idea to skim read the chapters. In the review, structure the material in paragraphs, as outlined above.

While you are doing this work, make notes of ideas (remember: complete sentences and not just key words), which you may use later. Write down questions to the text. Are some questions omitted, which the author should have posed? These questions and notes can be useful later when you are going to develop the topic and formulate your own research questions. Make a rule that whenever you find literature you think will be useful, write a summary of half a page to two pages. By now, you have begun writing the thesis. Most likely, you will end up writing more than you use in the final thesis; save the rest in a separate file, as you will perhaps use it for something else later.

Writing as a process

Good writing is primarily a question of practice. Writing is a process, and you will write several drafts before you have a final product. Once basic writing skills are learned, they must not be taken for granted. Just as with other skills, they must be maintained and used. Many students believe that their writing skills quickly improve if they attend a writing class. This is not necessarily true. You have to practise, seek critique, and get used to receiving critique. To be the student, the writer or the author you want to be, you must work continually to improve your writing.

3.5 Summary

1. Basic rules of writing are:
   - define the target audience
   - be aware of your personal investment in the topic
   - define the purpose of your writing.

2. Based on the audience for your writing, there are three different writing styles to choose from:

    - persuasive writing
    - compulsory writing
    - uninvited writing.

3. The structure of a paragraph:

    - topic sentence, inclusive of a controlling idea
    - clarifying sentence
    - propositions
    - supporting sentences
    - contrast and comparisons
    - concluding sentence stating findings and conclusions.

4. Tricks to continue writing include:

    - practise writing
    - use the brainstorming method
    - stop while you have good ideas
    - begin early with the research literature review
    - look at writing as a process.

5. Note the importance of studying good examples of a given writing style when you are attempting to improve your skills. It is a good idea to try to copy the style of a good author. There is a difference in copying a writing style and copying and stealing ideas from others and presenting them as your own. If you want to be a good writer, study the style and approach of those who came before you. If you read and analyse the writing of well-known authors, you can build on their skills and develop your own.

3.6 Action plan

1. Write a five-page essay that is going to be sent to a newspaper. It should be persuasive on one of the topics below:

    - immigration/deportation
    - taxes
    - the educational grading system
    - retirement/pension plans
    - global warming
    - any topic of interest.

2. The general public is your audience. The purpose of the essay is to demonstrate your writing skills and your ability to narrow a wide topic to a few propositions

you can discuss. After you have chosen a topic, use the following process to write a draft:
- write down one or two concepts that are important for your topic
- find documentation about the topic that is based on research
- narrow the topic and write at least five sub-topics for your chosen topic.

3 Organize and group them to the best of your knowledge and according to their relative importance to the overall topic.
- Formulate one or more propositions you want to discuss.
- What would be the question of a person who supports the proposition?
- Which arguments would someone present who sees the world from a different viewpoint?
- What would be your response?
- Choose one or more of the propositions and find evidence to support or weaken it.
- Go back to your draft and contrast your findings with your propositions. If you found documentation to support some propositions, expand them further. Take out those for which you did not find supporting documentation. If you found contrary documentation, use it in your argumentation.
- Summarize the discussion and present your conclusion.

4
Who can help you? Establishing support networks

Doing research is not a solitary activity. Instead, research usually implies working with a number of people inside and outside the university campus. Professional and personal networking is an important aspect of writing a master's thesis. During the writing process, your network will primarily consist of fellow students and the faculty at your university. It is your responsibility to establish support networks. Some students feel that this is difficult, as they shy away from initiating professional contacts. The fact is that you need a network in order to write a thesis. You must talk with a professor to have a thesis advisor, and you will undoubtedly talk with people outside the campus to access data.

Professional and personal networking will also be of great significance after graduation. Several students establish friendship networks which they will draw upon throughout their careers. Many graduates also get jobs as a result of networking when they were students. Establishing professional and personal networks is essential while writing your thesis.

4.1 Social media

We will begin by talking about social media. This does not mean that we think that social media replaces face-to-face interactions with students, advisors and others. Nevertheless, social media plays a major role in establishing and maintaining personal and professional networks. For example, many universities have Facebook profiles, which often include alumni (www.facebook.com). Further, LinkedIn is important when establishing a professional network (www.linkedin.com). Academia also serves as a social meeting place in the same way as Facebook does, but it is directed at academics (www.academia.edu). Many forms of social media are useful for more than just finding and maintaining networks; you can participate in current debates, search for information, follow the latest research and find job openings.

Many students find social media to be useful during different phases of writing a master's thesis. You may ask if someone has information about books and articles on given topics. Some students use social media to get in touch with informants for interviews or a survey. Even if social media is not ideal for long conversations, you can test ideas or propositions. By posting your view on an issue, you will receive many questions and opposing views. When people from different disciplines participate, the debate will often develop further as concepts are defined, new knowledge is acquired and new ideas are presented. You can also communicate the findings of your research as you go along. You will be surprised how many people are interested in research findings. Many students use social media as a support system, for example when working on the thesis feels lonely and you are struggling with data collection, structure, analysis and deadlines. A sigh from a frustrated or tired student will usually result in 'Likes' and words of comfort from others who struggle with similar issues. It is important to create a profile and be active in social media in order to draw from this well of knowledge and support. Use them to establish and maintain local, national and international professional networks.

Finally, many students are blogging when they are writing a master's thesis. Blogging might help you to establish a support network where you share experiences and receive information and tips from readers and other bloggers.

4.2 Students

As noted, networking with other students is useful during several phases of writing a thesis. When you are trying to find a topic, it is helpful to discuss different options with others. They can also be a great resource when searching for relevant research literature. Students often help each other by reading early outlines and giving critique. This is useful even if you work on different topics. Perhaps some issues are underdeveloped and need more work. By letting someone else read your work, you will get used to receiving critique. Getting critique and suggestions for improvements are important in all aspects of academic work. Most students feel that this is challenging, usually because they are not used to it. Finally, you will get help in improving your language. Perhaps you make systematic mistakes, which a good reader will discover and point out to you.

Many professors observe a certain degree of jealousy among students. Some hesitate to share information, tips and experiences in the belief that this will give them a cutting edge over the others. However, unwillingness to provide information and help to fellow students will often result in isolation when other students decline giving you help when you need it. Also, the student who receives help is not the only one to reap the benefits; by reading the work of others, you learn a lot in the process. When you read a text someone else has written, you will improve the ability to analyse text. This will be helpful in your own writing.

Assessing the writing of fellow students

Some students have little experience with commenting on the written work of others. Here, we will give a few ideas. A common rule is to use examples from the text to illustrate your critique. Remember to include suggestions for how to improve the text. It is important that you first outline the positive aspects of what you have read. This helps the other student to stay motivated. If you are too negative, the other student will either lose the desire to write or lose the desire to show you something later.

Also assess their structure and technique. Relatively simple issues can be addressed. Are the headings short and easy to understand? Is the draft paginated? How does the student reference and use the research literature? Is the reference list written according to accepted format and style? Is the text systematic and easy to follow, or is it poorly organized? Assess the language too. Are many sentences general and lacking precision? Or are they complicated and pretentious? Are the sentences too long? What about the punctuation?

Assessing the content is the most challenging part. Your ability to give good comments depends on your knowledge in the field. It is difficult to see if all the key issues are addressed when you know little or nothing about the topic. However, even if your knowledge is limited, you can assess the presentation of the content. Is the argumentation convincing? Can you think of other arguments or issues that should be included? Is the reasoning logical and consistent?

Finally, conclude with encouragements. Remember that you want the other students to maintain a desire to write. The student who lets you read her or his work should end up with a feeling that this text can be improved. By working closely with other students, there will always be someone to share your joy when the writing goes well. You will also have someone to talk to when the writing seems to go nowhere. Perhaps most important of all, you can make a difference to someone else's life.

4.3 The advisor

Your advisors are important persons during the process of writing a master's thesis. In the following we will write about the advisor in singular, although some students have a co-advisor in addition to their main advisor. Most universities have university and course-level guidance and procedures that students are expected to follow when it comes to the appointment or selection of the advisor and in case of difficulties. The practical and ethical responsibilities we discuss in this chapter are also closely linked to professional body ethical guidelines (see section 1.3). Read these guidelines and get to know the ethical principles and codes of conduct that are relevant for you.

Here, we want to discuss some aspects of the student–advisor relationship. Before we begin, we would like to remind you that the final *responsibility* for the master's thesis is not that of your advisor, but yours alone. This means that you must make sure you have an advisor who works well with you. This also means that you must take action if you feel that your relationship with the advisor does not function according to your expectations.

4.4 The responsibilities of advisors and students

We will take a look at some areas of responsibility for advisors and students. Perhaps this will clarify a few potential difficult areas and help you avoid the most common traps. Let us first take a look at the advisor before we turn to the responsibilities of the student.

The advisor's responsibilities

The faculty at a university has the necessary *academic qualifications* to advise students in writing a master's thesis. Some students might be concerned and wonder if a given advisor has detailed expert knowledge within the particular field they are writing. Strictly speaking this is not necessary, as most advisors are good generalists within their disciplines. Nevertheless, when you talk with a potential advisor, she or he should recognize their ability to advise you and whether you need to seek further expertise elsewhere. If the advisor lacks specific knowledge in your particular field, you may be able to use a co-advisor who does have the required expertise.

All advisors have *ethical responsibilities* towards students. Most universities have specified ethical guidelines for faculty that are available online. Check with your university to see what they are. Here we will briefly describe some common ethical guidelines for advisors. First, advisors must demonstrate respect for the challenges that the advisor role offers and try to be a role model for their students. Second, advisors must demonstrate respect for the students' personal and professional integrity. This means that advisors must, through their attitude, language and action, show respect for the student's gender, ethnicity, age, sexual orientation, worldview, disability or intellectual ability. In other words, advisors have the responsibility to treat students with respect and equality, and never harass or discriminate against students in any area.

Furthermore, advisors must be aware of the asymmetry in the advisor–student relationship. Students are to a certain degree dependent upon the advisors, and advisors cannot take advantage of students for their own personal or professional gain. Advisors should maintain a professional distance from their students and avoid double relationships that might cause conflicts of interest, like a romantic relationship or common economic interests. Advisors should not use the time with the student to discuss their own problems, but be sensitive to the student's own situation. Advisors should also be careful when talking about a colleague or student, and not cast aspersions.

If advisors want to use student data or research results, permissions to do so must be obtained from the students. Advisors must use the same rules of conduct for students as for fellow academics in referencing and crediting the work of others. Advisors should not receive any gifts or money from students apart from the payment from the university, and should consider carefully the consequences if accepting gifts or services from students. Finally, advisors should be willing to involve a second person if the relationship with the student becomes so difficult that further cooperation seems impossible.

Many popular advisors have little available time. Try to find an advisor who is *available* and who is not overloaded with students. Advisors must make sure they have time to prepare, which usually means to read your written text and to meet up with you. Advisors must also give you information about where and when they can meet. The worst situation for a student is to have an advisor who does not answer emails and is unavailable. Avoid such advisors if possible as they only cause frustrations. Occasionally advisors may be forced to change their appointment with you. Always check your email before your appointment to avoid any misunderstandings.

Advisors have a duty to *follow up* on your work. More specifically, the advisor must read your written work and point out its strengths and weaknesses. The response of a good advisor is so specific that you know what to do next. Unfortunately, some advisors are vague, which usually causes confusion. If this is your experience, ask the advisor to be specific. Advisors also have a responsibility for *the progress of your thesis*. Towards the end of every meeting, make an agreement on what you should do next, the date you send new or revised text, as well as the time and place for the next meeting.

The student's responsibilities

Our first advice might be unusual, but it is fundamental that you respect the advisor's expertise. It is frustrating for the advisor to give assignments and advice to students who refuse to follow them. This does not mean that you have to agree with the advisor in everything. If there is something you do not understand, let her or him know, so that misunderstandings are avoided. If you disagree, express your views so that the communication between you and your advisor becomes a constructive dialogue.

Good advisors give assignments to their students. Your advisor might ask you to read specific books or articles before the next meeting, or perhaps you need to check issues relating to data collection. If you fail to do these assignments, you are actually communicating that the professor's advice is not a priority and that you have no intention of following them. It is your job to let the advisor know if the workload is too heavy. Talk with the advisor and come to an agreement on what is a reasonable amount of work for you.

Before meeting your advisor, prepare by sending written text, for example a thesis outline, a chapter or parts of a chapter. Talk with the advisor and set a deadline, so that the advisor has time to read it properly before you meet. When you send the text, you may add questions or topics you want the advisor to pay attention to and address during the next meeting. Some students also write down questions they bring to the meeting and ask in person.

During the meeting, make sure you listen to what the advisor says. Let the advisor finish talking without interruptions, especially interjections like 'Yes, but …'. Put all defensive speech aside. When you are defending yourself, you are busy thinking about what you are going to say and not listening to what the advisor is actually saying. Instead, be an active listener and make notes. After the meeting, reflect critically on the advice you were given. Even if you do not follow it in every detail, remember to pay attention to the advice given. For example, if the advisor tells you that your discussion lacks substance and points to a particular paragraph to illustrate, you may disagree regarding this particular paragraph; nevertheless, ask yourself if the advisor might be right, and re-read your draft with this critique in mind.

End the meeting by making an agreement concerning the assignment for next time. The assignment should be specific, for example finishing one or more chapters or sections. Make sure you stick to the agreement. Most professors have little time, and it is important that you respect the advisor's time by communicating if something comes up that prevents you from doing the assignment or coming to the meeting.

Some students like to write a short summary after the meeting, which they share with the advisor by sending an email. They reiterate the critique of the previous assignment, the new assignment, the deadline for sending it, and the time and place for the next meeting. This might be of help in avoiding misunderstandings.

When the advisor–student relationship encounters difficulties

In some cases, the advisor–student relationship does not work. There could be many reasons. Sometimes, advisors and students disagree on substantial issues when it comes to the thesis itself. In other cases, advisors and students do not communicate very well. Perhaps the advisor gives superficial and vague comments, or perhaps the student does not follow up on what the advisor suggests. If you find yourself in this situation, it is important that you take action. The question is what to do. Most universities have guidance and procedures that students would be expected to follow in the case of difficulty with their advisor. Find out what they are and follow them. Here we will try to give you some additional advice, as there may not be one 'right' answer to every situation and the best outcome might be when the least harm is done to all involved.

Try to analyse the situation. Why do you have difficulties with the advisor? Are there more basic academic disagreements or differences that cause the difficulties? Are there practical issues that need be addressed? Or are there fundamental ethical issues involved, such as discrimination or harassment? The answer to these questions will largely determine further action. If the latter causes difficulties, it is important that you follow the university guidance and procedures. Do not try to resolve these issues on your own.

If you want to talk with the advisor to resolve the situation, remember that the most effective problem solving happens in a neutral tone. Try to stay emotionally objective and do not distribute guilt and blame. If you do, the advisor will most likely take a defensive stance. A far better approach is to specify what your needs are. Say, for example, that you need more specific and detailed comments on your work, and ask if this is possible. In this way, you direct the attention towards your own needs rather than the shortcomings of the advisor. This approach increases your chances of being heard. Look for solutions that are acceptable for both of you.

In some cases, the differences are more fundamental. If this is your situation, it might be a good idea to contact your university for problem-solving advice. If the solution is to find a new advisor, the university will help you with this process. In some cases, the solution might be to find a co-advisor, if this is permitted within institutional rules. In doing so, you do not address the problems directly, but use the co-advisor as a main advisor and vice versa.

Finally, there are situations where students want to switch advisors simply because they found other advisors with more expert knowledge than their present one. In this case, it should be relatively uncomplicated to explain the situation to the present advisor, but contact the university beforehand to see if it is possible to switch advisors for this reason.

4.5 Summary

1. Professional and personal networking is an important aspect of writing a thesis.
2. Being active in social media helps to build local, national and international professional networks.
3. Networking with other students is useful during several phases of writing a thesis.
4. Most universities have university and course-level guidance, and procedures that students are expected to follow when it comes to the appointment or selection of the advisor and in the case of difficulties. Read these guidelines and follow them.
5. Advisors have academic and ethical responsibilities towards students.
6. Students have responsibilities to follow up on their work and communicate with the advisor.
7. The final responsibility for the thesis is not that of your advisor, it is yours alone.

4.6 Action plan

1. Create a profile with relevant social media and maintain an active presence.
2. Make a list of the people you think can be of support when writing your master's thesis. Talk to people you already know and ask them to help you.
3. Find out as much as possible about the people on your list. What are their research interests? What have they published? Which courses have they taught? Information about the people you contact is helpful when you talk to them and try to motivate them to work with you.
4. Take the initiative to form a student group within a specific topic or field. Create a social agenda around the group.
5. Collect information about potential advisors for your thesis.
6. Start contacting potential advisors. Perhaps you need to talk to more than one before you find the one(s) who actually end up being your advisor(s).

5
A guide for searching the literature[1]

This chapter outlines different aspects of searching the literature. We will take a look at why searching the literature is important, and the different ways in which the research literature is used in a master's thesis. It is helpful to be familiar with different types of literature and how to locate literature at the library and online. You will also find information about identifying useful books and articles and making a record of your search.

5.1 Why search the literature?

An essential part of all research is a search of the research literature. A basic principle for all research, including a master's thesis, is that it is a collective enterprise. You need to begin with the knowledge that other people have acquired. This means that you must become familiar with your topic. Another important principle in research is to develop the topic further by contributing some sort of new knowledge. When a master's thesis is finished, we should know something we did not know before you began your work. Searching the literature is related to both principles.

The research literature on your topic will include different kinds of material, such as books, articles, theses and research reports. Searching and reading

---

[1]Thanks to Mark Janes, Social Sciences Subject Consultant, Bodleian Libraries, University of Oxford, and Ragnhild Sundsbak, Subject Librarian of Political Science at the University of Oslo Library, who have helped to edit and update the information about search methods, bibliographic databases, types of publication and keeping a search log.

the literature can be time consuming. It is, therefore, important to begin searching the literature early (see sections 1.1 and 3.4). In some master's theses, the description and the discussion of the research literature seem disconnected from the rest of the thesis; the reader is left with the impression that the literature was read after the analysis was finished. If you start too late with literature searching and analytical reading, the thesis will tend to be fragmented. Finding and analysing the literature early in the writing process has important intellectual and practical value. A critical analysis of the literature will help you create continuity between the literature and the rest of the thesis. It will also lead to new insights and analytical tools that are useful in the empirical analysis. By searching and reading research literature throughout the entire thesis process, you will have time and space to distinguish between relevant and irrelevant literature, and significant and insignificant literature. This approach will enable you to draw on the literature in all parts of the thesis.

The purpose of reviewing research literature is twofold. First, your job is to demonstrate to the reader that you know and understand how other scholars have approached your topic. Searching the literature will help you identify research that is relevant to your thesis. Second, reviewing the literature prevents you from addressing outdated topics or answering questions that have already been answered by someone else. If you are not up to date with current research, you may risk duplicating what someone else has already done. This is definitely a situation you want to avoid.

5.2 How to use the literature in your thesis

The purpose of the literature review is to describe and analyse the knowledge that exists about a problem that concerns you. This knowledge may have the character of theory, empirical studies or methods. You need to know the research that has been conducted on your topic and how it is studied. The research literature will benefit your thesis by providing new and relevant insight. Here we will give an outline of how to use it in different parts of your thesis.

To find a topic

When you have selected an area within your discipline that interests you, reading the research literature will help you to identify a more specific topic for your thesis (see section 1.1). Perhaps you find a scholarly debate that catches your attention and you want to pursue. Or you find neglected areas in previous research, in the sense that they do not address or explain phenomena the way you think they should. Sometimes students find information about international studies they want to replicate in their own country. Most research literature concludes with suggestions for further research, and these suggestions might give you new ideas.

To construct a theoretical framework

A common problem in many master's theses is that there are few connections between theory and empirical findings. In order to create continuity and relevance between theory and the empirical study, your must place your work within a larger framework. What have other scholars done on your topic? How have they approached the topic? Which theoretical frameworks did they use? A critical analysis and synthesis of existing research often leads to new knowledge. Use the research literature to construct a theoretical framework and place your work in the context of previous research (see section 6.1).

In some instances, it is easy to find theoretical frameworks that are useful for your topic. This is often the case if you have selected a topic where some work has already been done. In other instances, you need to use the lack of theoretical frameworks to create a space for your work. A critical analysis of previous research might lead you to conclude that current theoretical frameworks are insufficient for your research problem. This insight can be used to revise current theories, propose alternative ones or develop new ones.

To define key concepts

In some theses, the definition of key concepts is crucial to understanding the topic. The research literature provides different definitions of concepts and how they have developed over time. By defining key concepts, you clarify the meaning of the concepts in your thesis and define what is included and excluded (see section 1.2).

To frame and specify research questions

Use the literature to define a space that has been neglected by other researchers. When you describe how other researchers have approached your topic and how they framed their research questions, you will be able to find gaps in existing research. If the literature review is going to have this function, you need to limit the description and analysis of the research literature to your research questions. When you describe a theory or an empirical study, make sure the literature is relevant to the issues you are discussing. This form of literature review will help you specify your research questions (see section 7.4).

To give ideas for designing the methodology

The research literature, especially empirical studies, gives insight into methodological issues. It lets you know how other researchers have gone about the business of collecting the appropriate data (see section 8.2). It gives ideas about how to design the methodology for your project by identifying key issues, samples and data collecting methods. It will also give an awareness of possible methodological weaknesses and problems related to your topic.

To find strategies for analysis

It is always useful to know about and understand how other researchers have analysed your topic. It does not matter if the purpose of your thesis is to solve problems, describe a phenomenon, explain it or test hypotheses. We have mentioned before that studying good research is an important element in learning how to write a master's thesis (see section 3.5). We remind you again: you will learn how to write an academic text by studying and copying the approach and the style of a good researcher.

The research literature will give you ideas of how to go about writing a thesis. This is also true when it comes to the analysis (see section 9). In some instances, it is a good idea to use the same analytical strategies you find in a similar study. In other instances, use the research literature to find out why you do not want to analyse your data in a specific way. By using the literature to define why you do not want to pursue a form of analytical strategy, you justify an alternative strategy.

5.3 Where to begin and what to include

How much do I need to include in the literature review? Maybe it is impossible to answer this question, but there are some criteria that are useful to know. The minimum requirement for a book or article to be included is that it is relevant and important for your research questions. Further, it is important to include the most recent works in the field. This is where you will find the latest research findings. In some disciplines, it is a requirement that you include the classics in the discipline. You do this to demonstrate that you are well oriented in the discipline and its traditions. Classics are often discussed in current debates, and it is a good idea to reference these academic debates.

When am I going to start reading and where should I begin? We suggest that you begin with the secondary literature (i.e. general and subject encyclopaedias and dictionaries, subject bibliographies, journal articles, textbooks, research reports, master's theses and doctoral dissertations). Some ambitious students want to dive into the thinker's original literature. This can be time consuming, and if you start reading in the wrong place you may risk impeding your progress. It is a good idea to use the secondary literature when you begin to read in a new area. Once you have gained an overview of the secondary literature, it is time to start reading the original literature. We will give you more information about types of literature as we go along.

5.4 Surf on top or dive into the deep Web?

Students are used to finding information on the Internet by using search engines like Google (www.google.com) and the online encyclopaedia Wikipedia (http://en.wikipedia.org). It is easy to find information through these and other websites. The problem is, however, that many students unquestioningly use what they find on these websites. Accuracy of the data should be cross-checked. Also it is sometimes difficult to distinguish between relevant and irrelevant information.

You need to know that Google and other search engines only show you a small part of all the information available on the Internet. There is a lot of information you do not access by only using search engines, for example bibliographic databases (see section 5.6). When you are going to write a master's thesis, you are required to dig deeper and use more sources and more literature than what you find via search engines. It is not sufficient to reference information you found on Wikipedia. In this chapter, we will show you how to locate material and literature that you can use in a master's thesis.

5.5 Methods for searching literature

Many students think that searching and locating the relevant literature is easy. It is true that an electronic search will quickly give you access to databases as well as a huge number of websites. However, there is so much information out there that it is easy to get overwhelmed.

When you are going to begin searching the literature, our first advice is that you talk with your advisor and fellow students. People who know you and what you are looking for can give you good ideas for getting started. At the academic library, there are specialists within different disciplines – subject librarians. Talk to them and ask for help. Further, references in articles and textbooks are important places to start.

We will give you advice about electronic searches. The information given here is rather introductory, but more information can be found in other literature (see Hart, 2008b). First and foremost, when you find books, journals and articles you think are relevant, you must save the findings electronically or print them out together with detailed information about where you found them (see section 5.9). It is sometimes extremely difficult or almost impossible to go back and locate literature you have found earlier.

Books for sale

Searching the literature primarily takes place on the Internet and in the library. Sometimes you will want to buy books rather than borrow them, so we will begin here. First of all, you need to know which books are available for purchase. The easiest way to find this out is to search in an Internet book store. You can look at Amazon (American and English) and WHSmith (English). If you are interested in out of print or used books, you can find them through Internet bookstores that specialize in this type of literature. At AbeBooks, for example, you can buy books from several stores (www.abebooks.co.uk). Another way to find books is to search Google Books, which provides a unique full-text search within the books (http://books.google.com).

Information about books for purchase can also be found in various catalogues that academic book stores and libraries will have. It is possible to search using the publication's title or author. *Whitaker's Books in Print* (1988–) published in the UK, or *Global Books in Print* (1948–) and *Subject Guide to Books in Print* (1957–) published in the US are the most central. *Global Books in Print* is also available online (www.globalbooksinprint.com) – find out if your library subscribes to this resource.

In addition, search the publisher's website. Most publishers produce catalogues and give information about present and forthcoming publications. These catalogues can often be searched online. Some publishers also include information about books from other publishers.

The library

Books and articles are the sources of material used by most researchers. When you search the literature at the library, you need to know how the library is organized and how to retrieve information in the catalogues and databases to access the collections. Since the available amount of data is enormous, you need help to find what you want and to sort the relevant literature from the irrelevant. It is a good idea to attend a class arranged by the library for new users. By getting to know the search engines and library catalogues, you will have an overview of the available information and acquire the skills to search on your own. Learning to use the library's resources early on helps you to be more effective, which will save you time and unnecessary frustrations. If the library is busy, search the literature at times when fewer people are there, either early in the morning or late in the afternoon or evening.

On the university library's website, many subject librarians have their own pages. Find the librarian within your discipline and visit their site on a regular basis. There you will find information about new books, journals and important databases. You will also find information about classes.

When you want to find out where the books and the journals within your discipline are located, take a tour of the university library. In order to do so, you need to know how the books and the journals are classified. The most popular system of classification in the UK and many other countries is the international Dewey Decimal Classification (DDC). In the US, it is the Library of Congress Classification. The Dewey system organizes books according to subject content. For example, literature within the social sciences are placed under 300. The system is further arranged in a hierarchy according to the principle *from general to specific*. This means that the subjects are subdivided on different levels into specific subject content. The second level of subdivisions for the 300s is, for example, 320 Political Science, 330 Economics, 340 Law, 350 Public Administration, 360 Social Services and so on.

Be aware that there might be more than one location for a given subject. For example, the subject 'children' has several locations, dependent upon the relative aspect of this subject. Also, a specific subject within the social sciences can be located according to another subject content. One example is Political History 900–909, 930–990, which is placed under 900 Geography, history and auxiliary disciplines. The printed and electronic registers in the libraries will show you the location.

By knowing the structure of the classification system and the form of a subject, you can follow leads and navigate your own way around a particular subject. The ability to start at one end and follow leads through is important for finding research literature. If you have difficulties finding a particular subject, ask the librarians for help.

Electronic search

Electronic media have created great opportunities in finding an enormous amount of literature. When you search for books electronically, you begin with a search of the library Online Public Access Catalogue (OPAC), an electronic library catalogue. You can search the OPACs of many libraries on the Internet. At most university libraries OPACs are very easy to use. You can search in various ways. You can search by *key word, author, title, word in title* or *classification number*. You can choose different key words and combine them with other key words when you search. For example, if you were searching for 'terrorism', a key word search would give results or 'hits' for all books that have the word 'terrorism' in the title. Many other books might be relevant for terrorism, but not have the word in the title. This is why it is important to have a list of key words or phrases that you use when you search. A good search vocabulary for 'terrorism' could, for example, include the following key words: political violence, religious violence, terror attack, violent social movements, extremism, security. Perhaps you can think of additional key words.

Having a good search vocabulary also means to focus. If the key words are too general, you will get too many hits, which means you need to narrow the search. If you get hardly any hits, try to use subject dictionaries, thesauri and encyclopaedias to find useful key words. A good approach can be to use a general key word in combinations with synonyms.

An electronic search of the library OPAC has many benefits compared to a manual search. In a few minutes you will have references to several sources of information. It is also possible to search for words in a title and search for abstracts (not all databases provide abstracts). It is a good idea to print the complete bibliographic details as you search. If you have many references, save the search results in *MetaLib*, a gateway to a range of electronic resources and databases that are relevant to users of academic libraries. You will need a user-ID and password to be able to save your search results. Many university libraries also send lists of references via email, which does not require login. If a student wants to get information about new literature within a field, it is possible to create *RSS-feeds* so that a permanent search delivers directly the latest data to your email address. Many databases described later in this chapter have this facility. Finally, searching the research literature continues throughout the writing process and might change based on the information you collect as your work progresses.

There are some disadvantages to electronic searches of OPACs. The registration in the databases is inconsistent. Different databases provide various types of information about the references. Also, electronic searching has tended to include mostly recent books. This is changing but, in some instances, you must search manually to find older literature.

5.6 Bibliographic databases

Most academic libraries access national and international bibliographic databases that can be used to find books and articles on your topic. The main sources are the library OPACs and national and international databases. We will mention some important databases here, although these examples include only a few. As mentioned above, it is important to remember that various databases give different information about the literature that is registered in the base. Also, most bibliographic databases do not include articles in collected works. If the database is available online, we will include the URL in parentheses.

National bibliographic databases

The two national bibliographic databases in the English-speaking world are the British National Bibliography (BNB) and the National Union Catalog (NUC) in the US. One of the largest collections of printed material is found in the British Library, with more than 17 million bibliographical records in several databases. Some of the material dates back to the 1500s. The BNB uses the Dewey system to classify entries and is available online (www.bl.uk). Copac is a national, academic and specialist catalogue of research libraries in the UK (http://copac.ac.uk). The NUC is based on the Library of Congress Catalog system and covers more than 20 million publications. It is available in many academic libraries outside the US.

Some important international databases

Several international bibliographic databases which reference books and journal articles are available online. Below, we will take a look at some of them. Ask for help at the library to access them. International databases surveille and register information in a number of languages. Even if an article is written in French, you will find it by using English key words, and the title is usually translated into English. When you search these databases, make sure you know the language in which the book or article is written, otherwise, you might end up ordering literature you are unable to read. Sometimes there are technical problems with the international databases. If you have problems with access, contact your local university library for help.

Google Scholar
Although Google Scholar is a search engine (see section 5.7) we will mention it here. Many students and researchers will start with Google Scholar when they are searching the literature (http://scholar.google.com). It is a resource that provides information on academic literature across several disciplines and from different sources, such as books, theses, articles and abstracts. Google Scholar is very easy to use. You will be able to find several different types of publications there and locate them through your library or on the Internet. The

documents are ranked by author, publisher and how recently they were cited in other research literature. However, this site does not encompass all publications in existence, so do not limit yourself to using this resource alone.

Scopus
Scopus is the largest abstract and citation database of peer-reviewed research literature and high-quality Web sources, through which you can search millions of abstracts and index data. Since abstracts, or summaries of the content of the publication, are included, it makes it easier for you to decide if the publication is relevant. However, institutional access is required, so you need a user-ID and password. Scopus is especially useful for economics, business, education, development and psychology.

JSTOR
Another very popular resource is JSTOR (Journal Storage), which has a large full-text collection of 'classic' academic journals. You can search digitized issues of hundreds of well-known journals. However, the most recent years are usually not available. Again, institutional access is required, and you need a user-ID and password.

Humanities International Index
There are numerous indexes for the different disciplines of published articles and reviews. The Humanities International Index database (www.ebscohost.com/corporate-research/humanities-international-index) is an index of articles and reviews in the humanities in American and English journals from 1974. It covers, for example, archaeology, history, classical studies, literature, languages, folklore, philosophy, religion, dance, film, theatre and music. The database provides key-word information on title, author, source, date of publication, language, key words and document type. The database has been available online since 1984. Institutional access is required, so you need a user-ID and password.

International Bibliography of the Social Sciences (IBSS)
IBSS is a multi-subject social science database that includes books and journal articles. It references publications from social anthropology, sociology, political science and economy. The printed edition covers the period 1953–1995. You can search in a database from 1981 through the library, even if there are some inconsistencies in the years before the millennium. Information is provided on title, author, source, document type, date of publication, language, key words and discipline.

IBSS, Sociological Abstracts (see below) and several other social science databases have been acquired by ProQuest and put on a new platform (http://search.proquest.com). This is a huge resource for social scientists.

Sociological Abstracts

In some cases the subject databases include abstracts or summaries of the content of the publication. Sociological Abstracts is an international database that collects and registers abstracts of journal articles, books, PhD dissertations and conference proceedings within sociology and related disciplines from 1952. The benefit of accessing the abstracts is that it makes it easier for you to decide if the publication is relevant. Sociological Abstracts is updated five times a year. Only publications since 1963 are searchable online. There are similar databases for other social science disciplines, for example Psychology Abstracts. In Sociological Abstracts, information is provided on title (with English translation), author, author's institution and address, journal, document type, language, place and date of publication, and a summary of content in English.

Historical Abstracts

This database collects and registers abstracts and journal articles within the historical disciplines and related topics in the humanities and the social sciences from 1952. It covers the entire world with the exception of the US and Canada. The bibliography is available online from 1973. The information includes document type, date of publication, key words, author, title, title translation in English, journal, abstract in English and historical period (historical period, historical period starting, historical period ending). Again, institutional access is required, so you need a user-ID and password.

Educational Resources Information Center (ERIC)

ERIC (from 1966) is a bibliographic database within education. ERIC is available online at the library and consists of Current Index to Journals in Education (CIJE) with references to articles in journals and Resources in Education (RIE) with references to different types of material. ERIC is international with an emphasis on the US.

Citation indexes

There are several other bibliographic databases that provide various forms of information. One database that is different from the others we have looked at above is the so-called citation indexes. Here, you can search for specific authors or specific publications, for example a journal article, and find a list of the publications that later have referenced or cited the author or the article you searched initially, who is citing it and where it is cited. The idea is that references or citations in a publication will indicate subject relationships between current and previous publications. The citation indexes provide opportunities to trace how older publications are used in contemporary research. A much used and important index for journal articles is the

ISI-Web of Science (www.isinet.com), which is part of ISI-Web of Knowledge (http://wokinfo.com). The database is divided into different fields, for example Sciences Citation Index (natural sciences), Social Sciences Citation Index and Arts and Humanities Citation Index.

5.7 Different types of literature

As stated before, when you are going to study a new topic it is a good idea to begin with the quick reference materials, which consists of handbooks, encyclopaedias and subject dictionaries, before you read books and journal articles. The reference material can introduce you to new subjects and give you an overview of the subject by clarifying it and providing facts about current research. These publications are located in the quick reference section in the academic library.

Handbooks

If you want to have a broad and compact overview of a topic or a subject, it is helpful to take a look at a recent handbook within your discipline. Handbooks are reference sources. They include articles that provide updated reviews of the research on a subject or discipline. Often, the articles include an extensive bibliography. The disadvantage of handbooks is that the research they reference is usually a couple of years older than the publication date. Some examples of handbooks are:

The Sage Handbook of Cultural Analysis (2008)

Handbook of Development Economics (2009)

The Oxford Handbook of the Sociology of Religion (2009)

Handbook of Social Psychology (2010)

The Oxford Handbook of Political Science (2011)

The Oxford Handbook of Philosophy of Mind (2011)

The International Handbooks of Media Studies (2012)

General and national encyclopaedias

Printed and electronic general encyclopaedias are useful for getting a first overview. In the English-speaking world, *Encyclopaedia Britannica* (2010) and *Encyclopedia Americana* (2009) are the largest ones. *Encyclopaedia*

Britannica (2010) is available online at the library. In the German-speaking world, *Brockhaus Enzyklopädie in 30 Bänden* (1986–2009) is important, which exists in an updated version online. In French, Larousse's *La grande encylopédie (1982–)* is highly regarded; an updated version is online and free. Whereas encyclopaedias used to be updated infrequently, several are now online, for example *Compton's Interactive Encyclopedia* and *Grolier Multimedia Encyclopedia*. A free online library and research encyclopaedia is *Encyclopedia.Com*, which is a reference source for students and researchers offering free articles, pictures and facts (www.encyclopedia.com). If you are not sure if you will be able to access an encyclopaedia, ask for help at the library.

Subject encyclopaedias and dictionaries

The subject encyclopaedias and dictionaries can be very useful resources for finding information about new topics. The main difference between an encyclopaedia and a dictionary is that an encyclopaedia will provide descriptions and a dictionary will give definitions. However, there is a fluid boundary between these two forms of publication, since many dictionaries provide as extensive information as encyclopaedias. Students within the social sciences should be familiar with *International Encyclopedia of the Social and Behavioral Sciences* (2001). The predecessors were *International Encyclopedia of the Social Sciences* (IESS) (1968–91) and *Encyclopedia of the Social Sciences* (1930–35). Generally, the more updated the encyclopaedia the more current the content. However, if you are interested in older time periods, ideas and theories, do not overlook some of these older encyclopaedias. *International Encyclopedia of the Social and Behavioral Sciences* is more extensive than the previous editions and consists of 26 volumes (it is also available as an online resource published by Elsevier). Several individual disciplines have encyclopaedias and dictionaries that cover subject-specific topics, theories and concepts. Many of these have extensive bibliographies and are indexed. Examples are:

Westermann Lexikon der Geographie (1968–72)

The Blackwell Companion to Sociology of Religion (2001; online via Blackwell Reference Online)

An Encyclopedia of World History, Ancient, Medieval, and Modern: Chronologically Arranged (2002)

A Dictionary of Modern Politics (2002)

The New Palgrave Dictionary of Economics (2008, also online)

Dictionary of Human Geography (2009)

Dictionary of Sociology (2009)

The Cambridge Dictionary of Christianity (2010)

The International Encyclopedia of Education (2010)

Concise Dictionary of Social and Cultural Anthropology (2011)

A somewhat different publication is *The Annual Register: A Record of World Events* (from 1758), which is the oldest of its kind in the world. It gives annual overviews of the political and economic situation around the world from a British perspective. It is produced annually in hardback and is also published electronically by ProQuest. Its archive is also available online from the publisher. *The Annual Register* was collected under the Internet Library of Early Journals project, a digital library administered by the universities in Birmingham, Leeds, Manchester and Oxford. The project finished in 1999 and no new entry admitted. The librarians at the library will help you find the type of subject encyclopaedia and dictionary you need.

Subject bibliographies

It is also a good idea to take a look at the main types of subject bibliographies found in the quick reference section at the library. These books contain entries that provide overviews of literature from all over the world on specific disciplines or subjects. Some subject bibliographies focus on specific disciplines. Examples are:

International Bibliography of the Social Sciences: Economics (2002)

Mass Media: A Bibliography with Indexes (Martin, 2002)

British Education Index (2003)

Cultural Anthropology: A Guide to References and Information Sources (2007)

International Bibliography of Historical Sciences (2009)

Other subject bibliographies are limited to specific subjects, for example *Women's Studies: A Recommended Bibliography* (Krikos and Ingold, 2004), *Gay and Lesbian Aging: Research and Future Directions* (Vries and Herdt, 2004) and *Index Islamicus* (2009). Some subject bibliographies are national bibliographies, for example *France* (1990), *England* (1993) and *Slovakia* (2000), published in *World Bibliographical Series* by Clio Press. Finally, some bibliographies are biographical, for example *Nineteenth-Century British Women Writers: A Bio-Bibliographical Sourcebook* (Bloom, 2000). *Oxford Bibliographies Online* is a new addition to this genre (www.oxfordbibliographies.com).

Journals

Thousands of academic journals are published every year. Most of them are published by commercial publishers in cooperation with academics who function as editors and editorial boards. Many journals are also connected to academic organizations. One example is *American Sociological Review* (from 1936), which is the journal of the American Sociological Association (ASA). Most academic libraries access a wide range of journals. If you are not sure which journal is relevant to your research, take a look at the library's journal collection. Use the library OPAC to get an overview of the journals that are available.

Many journals focus primarily on a specific discipline. Some of the most important journals in sociology are *American Journal of Sociology* (1895–), *American Sociological Review* (1936–) and *British Journal of Sociology* (1950–). In political science, *American Political Science Review* (1906–), *American Journal of Political Science* (1956–) and *Political Science Quarterly* (1886–) are important. *American Journal of Psychology* (1887–), *The Journal of Psychology* (1945–), *Journal of Clinical Psychology* (1945–) and *Journal of Personality and Social Psychology* (1910–) are considered influential in psychology. So are *American Anthropologist* (1888–), *Anthropological Quarterly* (1921–) and *Current Anthropology* (1959–) in social anthropology, and *The Economic Journal* (1891–), *Quarterly Journal of Economics* (1886–) and *American Economic Review* (1911–) in economics. We have only mentioned a few here. There are several other important journals within the different social science disciplines.

Many journals are multidisciplinary. One example is *Social Forces* (1922–), which focuses on sociology but publishes articles from social psychology, anthropology, political science, history and economics. Another example is *Gender and Society* (1987–), which includes articles on gender within all the social sciences. Other examples are: *Ethnic and Racial Studies* (1977–), *Studies on Crime and Crime Prevention* (1991–), *Journal of Conflict Resolution* (1957–), *Journal of Peace Research* (1964–) and *Journal for the Scientific Study of Religion* (1961–). Some journals also focus on area studies, such as *Journal of Near Eastern Studies* (1884–), *Harvard Journal of Asiatic Studies* (1936–), *African Studies* (1921–) and *Journal of Latin American Studies* (1969–).

Very useful for social scientists is a journal series called *Annual Review*. It consists of several review articles with extensive bibliographies that summarize 'the state of the art' in specific disciplines. They are helpful when searching for information on a new topic. Examples are: *Annual Review of Anthropology* (1972–), *Annual Review of Sociology* (1975–), *Annual Review of Political Science* (1932–), *New Geography* (1966/67–), *Annual Bulletin of*

Historical Literature (1911–) and *Journal of Economic Literature* (1963–). The review is updated and commented, and it gives cross-references to other disciplines.

Several journals are available online. In some cases you will find only abstracts and contents, but in other cases you will find the full article. Many articles are only available if your library has a subscription, which means that you need a user-ID and password. However, some electronic journals are 'open access' and free. One example is *Diversities* (www.unesco.org/shs/diversities), an interdisciplinary journal on diverse societies, published by UNESCO. Ask at the library how to find out which journals are available from your own computer and which are available via the library's homepage.

Some publishers also offer academic journal databases online, which give access to all the academic journals published by that publisher, for example *Sage Journals* (http://online.sagepub.com) and *Taylor & Francis Journals* (www.tandf.co.uk/journals).

Journal articles

It is in academic journals that you will find the most recent research on any given topic. Some journals provide useful review articles with extensive bibliographies. In the databases, these articles are usually classified as either 'feature article' or 'review article'. Pay attention to these articles when you begin searching the literature.

Efficient ways of finding journal articles are to study the bibliography of a recently published article on your topic and use indexes and abstracts (see section 5.6). Most journal articles are indexed and many are subject to abstracting services. It is quite common that academic journals are covered by more than one indexing and abstracting service. You can search in these international reference databases on subject, title, author and journal. If you are not sure which indexing and abstracting services are relevant to you, subject librarians should be able to help you. If the article is not in your library, the librarian can help you to order a copy.

Research methods

Books on research methods are useful during several phases of the thesis process, finding and developing a topic, selecting one or more methods and analytical strategies. There are a large number of books on research methods in the social sciences, but we would like to mention two book series here that provide a brief guidance with references to different methods. *Sage Little Green Books* series focuses on quantitative methods in the social sciences, whereas *Sage Little Blue Books* series teaches qualitative methods. You can also search *Sage Research Methods Online*, which is a tool to help researchers and students (http://srmo.sagepub.com).

Textbooks

Many textbooks give a general overview of a topic, the main ideas and the most influential authors in the discipline. Textbooks are also used for interdisciplinary work when you are not already familiar with the field. This information can provide a starting point for your search, but textbooks are seldom sufficient as sources of literature at master's level.

Research reports and current research

There are numerous research centres and research institutes that conduct all types of research. It can be very useful to see if someone is doing research on your topic so that you can contact them, inform them about your project, ask them for advice, and use them as part of your support network (see Chapter 4). These centres and institutes list overviews of current and past research programmes on their websites, including their research reports. The reports are often available free of charge in PDF files.

Several library OPACs will also have information about research reports that are published by various research centres and research institutes. On the library website, you will find information on databases where you can search alphabetically. Many libraries have the Current Research Information Systems (CRIS) database. This is a shared system for registration and reports of research and development activities for universities, colleges, research institutes, funders, media and the public. EuroCRIS was established to access current research information worldwide, but has an emphasis on Europe (www.eurocris.org).

Research councils also give information on current and previous research programmes and projects they fund and their outputs (books, journal articles and conference papers). The Economic and Social Research Council (ESRC) is one of the UK's seven research councils (see www.esrc.ac.uk). Another is the Arts and Humanities Research Council (AHRC) (www.ahrc.ac.uk). These research councils post research catalogues on their websites which list details of funded research projects and publications. You can search the catalogues by subject area, date, output type and key words. Likewise, the Social Science Research Council (SSRC) in the US posts links to programmes, projects, networks and events on their website (www.ssrc.org). You can also search their publication database, where you will find books, journal articles, event reports, working papers, multimedia content and so on.

Theses and dissertations

Completed master's theses and doctoral dissertations relevant for your topic can be very important sources of information. By taking a look at them, you will find the research status on your topic. They can give you ideas for a thesis topic, and they are useful sources of bibliographical references. At the library, theses and dissertations are usually placed in a separate collection. In the UK, unlike in the US, availability of theses varies as there are no systematic procedures for providing copies. Many universities store digital copies of theses which are accessed in a university open research archive (ORA). Here, the digital theses are open access and freely available online. In the UK and Ireland, an important way to search for relevant theses is to take a look at the ASLIB Index to Theses, which is a comprehensive listing of completed theses with abstracts (www.theses.com). In the US, search in the ProQuest Dissertations and Theses (PQDT) online databases which indexes, abstracts and provides full-text access to master's theses and PhD dissertations (www.proquest.com).

Official publications and statistics

Official publications and statistics can be important sources of data. Statistics are often used in many studies in social sciences, so it is important to know what data are available. UK National Statistics (www.statistics.gov.uk) and United States Census Bureau (www.census.gov) collect, analyse and publish statistical data on a wide range of topics. They produce catalogues of statistical sources on a regular basis, which are available for free online. You can browse the catalogues by theme or alphabetical order.

UK National Statistics publishes *Annual Abstract of Statistics* and *Monthly Digest of Statistics*, which are available free on their website. Another publication is the annual *Social Trends*, also available on their website, which includes articles that present social and economic data with explanations. The United Census Bureau also publishes a series of official publications as well as working papers which are available in PDF online.

Eurostat publishes statistical data of the European Union and candidate countries (http://epp.eurostat.ec.europa.eu). Eurostat also produces catalogues of statistical sources, which are available free online. You can search the catalogues by theme or alphabetical order. Eurostat publishes *Eurostat Yearbook* and *Eurostat Regional Yearbook*, which are available for purchase. When it comes to international statistics, there is another important yearbook, *The Europa World Yearbook* (1926–), which provides updated political and economic information about more than 250 countries and territories. An online version is available, but you need a user-ID and password.

Organizations like the United Nations (UN) (http://data.un.org), the World Bank (http://data.worldbank.org and https://openknowledge.worldbank.org), the Organization for Economic Co-operation and Development (OECD) (http://stats.oecd.org), and the World Health Organization (WHO) (www.who.int/gho/en) also provide information, publications and useful data on their websites.

We would also like to mention official and government publications and websites, such as Directgov, the official UK government website, where you will find references to material published by the different governmental departments and public bodies on a range of issues (www.direct.gov.uk). Likewise, USAGov provides a directory of the US government departments and agencies together with links. You will find overviews of white papers and propositions in full text, as well as lists of publications, research and reports (www.usa.gov). This information is updated daily.

In addition, parliamentary publications are available. The UK Parliament has an official website (www.parliament.uk), and so has the US Congress (www.congress.org). Here, you will find overviews of acts, bills, consultations, command papers, settings, documents and minutes. The benefit of using online access to official publications, documents and statistics is that you can search by theme or alphabetical order and find references to updated information. Many library OPACs have a website where these references are collected under the heading 'official publications'.

Newspapers

Most universities have subscriptions to digital archives of *The Times*, *The Economist*, *New York Times*, *Wall Street Journal*, *Washington Post*, *LATimes* and several other newspapers.

Many also subscribe to Factiva, a large database of news and business information with research tools (www.factiva.com), and LexisNexis, an electronic database for legal, public-records and journalistic documents (www.lexisnexis.com/en-us/home.page)

Conference proceedings and archives

There are several types of unpublished material that are available to the public. We have already mentioned unpublished theses and dissertations. The proceedings of conferences are also unpublished, as they consist of papers presented by the participants. Many professional organizations, like the American Sociological Association (ASA) or the British Psychological Association (BPA), hold annual conferences on specific themes. The proceedings of these conferences can give you 'state of the art' information. These associations will often publish the paper abstracts on their websites. You will be able to obtain a copy of papers given at past conferences by asking the associations or by emailing the author of the paper. You need to know the international index of conference proceedings, *Index to Social Sciences & Humanities Proceedings* (1979–), which indexes individual papers and can be searched by using key words, author and location.

We would also like to mention archives. There are thousands of archives with collections of unpublished text, data, documents, photos and so on. There are public and private archives, as well as national and international ones. There are also archives within different disciplines and topics. For example, the University of Michigan Government Documents Center has a very useful archive on Canadian and American politics, the UN and the EU. Some students want to use other forms of unpublished material which is not easily available, such as diaries and letters. If you are going to use this type of material, ask for help at the national library's manuscript collection.

The Internet

We have pointed out the enormous amount of data available on the Internet several times. The most challenging aspect of using the Internet when working on your master's thesis is to distinguish relevant from irrelevant information. It is important that you go to the deep Web and use some of the websites we have mentioned here, rather than surf on top and only use search engines, as different search engines structure and range the available websites. Nevertheless, we have already mentioned Google Scholar, which can be useful in your work because it gives you lists of scientific material with automatic access to your academic library's subscription. Most bibliographic databases, including Google Scholar, do not cover publications from non-governmental organizations (NGOs), intergovernmental organizations (IGOs), charities or policy institutes. Often Google and hunting through websites are the only options of finding them.

5.8 Identifying useful books and articles

When you find a book, a journal article or a website you need to judge its value and find out if it is important to your research. There is no fixed method of assessing the value of books and articles, but by looking at the following you will have a few criteria by which to distinguish between relevant and irrelevant material.

Author's name

If you recognize the name of the author as a scholar who is often referenced, there is a good chance that this author is a renowned authority in the discipline.

Title and subtitle

If the title or the subtitle has key words that are important for your research, take a closer look at the article or the book.

Journal name

Become familiar with the most important journals within your discipline. The name of a journal will help to you know the area it covers.

Publisher and place of publication

The most important publications are published by the large, well-known publishers, and they are usually published in cities where famous universities are located. However, you can also find relevant books published by smaller publishers.

Date of publication

It is a good idea to begin with recent publications, because they will reference older publications. By reading recent literature, you will get to know about the older literature that is relevant for your research.

Websites

A common problem with websites is that the credibility of the information is not guaranteed. Websites of established and well-known institutions have the same reliability and credibility as the institutions themselves. Get to know the websites of institutions that might be relevant for your thesis. Be more critical towards websites of new and unknown institutions, groups or persons.

Content

In order to select key literature, you need information about the content, especially if you are going to purchase books or order from other libraries.

This information is available in the databases for searching literature which provide abstracts or summaries of the publications. If the book or the article is referenced in a review article, it has been reviewed and approved by other scholars. Review articles provide information about key literature within a discipline or on a topic. Another possibility is to use book reviews found in academic journals. Some journals only publish book reviews. One example is *Book Review Digest* (1905–), which references and quotes book reviews taken from a selection of American, British and Canadian journals within the social sciences and the humanities. There are similar journals within different disciplines, for example *Reviews in Anthropology* (1974–), *International Review of Education* (1955–), *History: Review of New Books* (1972–) and *Contemporary Psychology: A Journal of Reviews* (1956–).

When you have obtained a copy of a book, you need to know if it is relevant for you without having to read the entire book. To judge the book, take a look at the following:

- *Text on the back cover:* a brief summary of the book.
- *Content's list:* a quick overview of the topics covered in the book and the priority given to each topic.
- *Preface:* information about the purpose of the book and the audience the author wants to reach.
- *Index:* an overview of the concepts used by the author and a quick way to see if they are appropriate to your topic. By looking up some important key words, you will see if the author discusses topics that are relevant for your work.
- *Bibliography:* lets you see if the author references scholars who are considered important for your work.
- *Skim reading:* by reading the first and last two sentences of a paragraph you will have an idea of the main content. Skim read sections of the book, or just the introduction and first chapter as this is where you will find information on the background of the book and the research questions. Then skim read the last chapter which presents a summary and conclusions.

5.9 How to keep a search log

When you are searching the literature, you will find a much larger amount of books and articles than you can possibly read at that time. It is extremely important that you keep some sort of record of your search. Management of the search is good project planning. Anyone who has tried to find a publication based on incomplete information knows how time consuming and frustrating this is. It is not so important what type of record you keep. You can produce an electronic search log, use prints and copies, or take handwritten notes. The important issue is that the system works for you. Below are some ideas of how to produce a log.

Endnote, Zotero, Mendeley and datafiles

An electronic search log can be made by using bibliographic systems or by making a search file on your computer. There is a range of software for constructing search logs, such as Endnote, Zotero and Mendeley. Endnote is a good and stable program for collecting references, while Zotero offers a solution that does not cost money. Mendeley is also free and very popular, and enables you to share your library (www.mendeley.com). Another alternative is to create a file on your computer. Whichever way you choose, it is very important that you keep accurate, consistent and correct records. Make sure you construct complete references including author, title, place of publication, publisher, date of publication and the location of the book (name of the library and classification number). A list of references can be systematized according to theme or alphabetical order based on the author's last name, or a combination of the two. When you search the databases previously mentioned in this chapter, you will often find that it is possible to import bibliographic data in different formats. They can be imported into a reference program or to your email, and then systematized according to your own need (see section 5.5).

Prints and copies

When you are searching literature electronically, and you think you are finding relevant literature, print the search details. If you find a large number of references, print them or save the search results in a file. It is sometimes a good idea to print or copy the front page and contents list of a book or a journal. Include the page that gives information about date and place of publication. As a safeguard, staple the pages together so that you know which information goes with what, and store in a simple ring binder.

5.10 A few useful websites

Archives

National Archives (UK): www.nationalarchives.gov.uk
National Archives of Australia: www.naa.gov.au
US National Archives: www.archives.gov

Internet bookstores

AbeBooks: www.abebooks.co.uk

Amazon: www.amazon.co.uk (UK) and www.amazon.com (US)

WHSmith: www.whsmith.co.uk

National libraries

The British Library: www.bl.uk

Library and Archives Canada: www.collectionscanada.gc.ca

Library of Congress: www.loc.gov

National Library of Australia: www.nla.gov.au

Official publications and statistics

Directgov: www.direct.gov.uk

Eurostat: http://epp.eurostat.ec.europa.eu

OECD Statistics: http://stats.oecd.org

UK National Statistics: www.statistics.gov.uk

UK Parliament: www.parliament.uk

United Nations: http://data.un.org

United States Census Bureau: www.census.gov

USAGov: www.usa.gov

US Congress: www.congress.org

WHO Global Health Observatory: www.who.int/gho/en

World Bank: http://data.worldbank.org and https://openknowledge.worldbank.org

Research councils

Arts and Humanities Research Council (AHRC): www.ahrc.ac.uk

Economic and Social Research Council (ESRC): www.esrc.ac.uk

Social Science Research Council (SSRC): www.ssrc.org

Search tools

Google: www.google.com

Google Books: http://books.google.com

Google Scholar: http://scholar.google.com

University of Michigan Government Documents Center: www.lib.umich.edu/govdocs/polisci.html

Theses and dissertations

ASLIB Index to Theses: www.theses.com

ProQuest Dissertations and Theses (PQDT): www.proquest.com/en-US/catalogs/databases/detail/pqdt.shtml

5.11 Summary

1. The purpose of reviewing literature is to demonstrate your knowledge and understanding of the topic and to prevent you from addressing outdated topics.
2. The research literature can be used to find a topic, construct a theoretical framework, define key concepts, frame and specify research questions, and develop ideas for methodology and strategies for analysis.
3. It is not sufficient to use search engines to find literature, you also need to search electronically through the library OPACs and databases.
4. The academic libraries arrange classes for new users every semester.
5. The materials in the quick-reference section of the library are a good place to start.
6. Several national and international bibliographic databases and services can be used to find books and articles.
7. Articles from refereed academic journals are a crucial source of information in any research. Recent publications and indexing and abstracting services provide the main tools to find articles.
8. Other important sources of information are research reports, theses and dissertations, official publications, statistics, newspapers, research methods books, textbooks, conference proceedings and archival material.
9. Produce a search log that keeps accurate, consistent and correct records.
10. A subject librarian will have knowledge of different types of literature and databases. They are there to help you.
11. Begin searching the literature early.
12. Essentially, reading leads to writing.

5.12 Action plan

Searching the literature is time consuming and you need to plan the search carefully. In order to find research literature it is important that you begin at one end and follow the leads. Start with a topic that interests you:

1. Talk with your advisor and fellow students to get ideas for relevant literature. People who know you and what you are looking for can help you to get started.
2. Sign up for a class for new users at the library. By getting to know the library catalogues and search engines, you will learn how the library works and to search on your own. Visit the website of the subject librarian in your discipline.
3. Find the relevant handbooks at the library. See if there is an annual review for your discipline. Look for general and subject dictionaries and encyclopaedias.
4. Browse the most important academic journals in your discipline to find information about recent research, who does what and how research is conducted.
5. Search for literature electronically. Experiment with different key words.
6. Try to find the most recent publications, where you will find the latest research results and references to older publications.
7. When you find a book, use the criteria mentioned in section 5.8 to see if it is useful for your work.
8. Keep a search log that works for you. Log all the publications you find and remember to include correct and complete information.

6
Reviewing research literature

About 20 per cent of your thesis should be set aside to review and discuss the research literature (see section 11.1). This is a good place to begin for many students, especially if you have problems getting started. The first section of the review consists of a presentation of relevant literature. By starting here you have begun the next important step, namely to discuss the research literature. We will describe both aspects here.

The purpose of the literature review is to define the space that has been neglected by other scholars. This helps to clarify and determine how original your contribution is. The first part of the literature review includes a description of the major contributions in the field, which are criticized and discussed in the second part. This strategy helps you develop the argumentation and establish a theoretical framework. By reviewing the research literature you will also obtain the necessary knowledge to formulate good research questions.

6.1 Coherence

The lack of coherence is a problem in many master's theses. In some instances, the reader has a feeling that the research literature was read after the research was done and written as a separate chapter to add credibility. There is nothing wrong with having a separate chapter devoted to literature, but it must be related to the subsequent research. Coherence in a thesis is established and maintained in much the same way as coherence in a paragraph (section 3.3). It is structured and organized according to an overall objective.

Coherence should be evident in several sections of the thesis. We will discuss this as we go along. However, here are a few reminders. In order to create coherence between theory and empirical facts, you must first use the research literature to establish a framework. Once you find or determine a particular scientific problem, it must be contextualized in relation to relevant research. It is your job to find the research that has been done, and how other scholars have studied similar topics. One example is a study of the role that foreign policy plays in American presidential elections, where the student reviewed the research both on broad analyses of voting decisions and more restricted analyses of the importance of foreign policy in the American public (Lian, 2010). This student used current research to create frameworks for his thesis.

Some students search for a theoretical framework they hope will fit their thesis perfectly. Such frameworks rarely exist. One reason may be that you approach a problem from a different angle than those who came before you. Or perhaps previous research does not pose the kind of questions you do or it suffers from neglect. In these situations, use the gaps in the research literature as a justification for your approach. By pointing out the weaknesses in current research, you define the space neglected by others.

Coherence must also be evident in the research questions. When you formulate a research question, it often constitutes a small part of a larger scientific problem. One example is the thesis on American presidential elections mentioned above, where the student asked: 'How important are opinions on foreign policy values and issues for American voters when determining their final vote in the general elections?' (Lian, 2010: 8). This question is related to larger scientific problems within political science, namely explaining voter decisions and election outcomes (ibid.: 10). The connection between the specific research question and the larger debates within your field must be present in the thesis. In Chapter 7, we will show you how to use the research literature to formulate research questions. It is by relating specific questions to a larger scientific problem that your thesis can contribute to new knowledge in the field.

Furthermore, there must be coherence between theory and analysis. Theories are meant to help you develop systems of interpretations and explanations, which you use in the analysis (see section 9). For example, when you present your findings, you need to compare them with findings in previous research. However, theories are not used solely as frames for interpretation of empirical data; you use the data to criticize and modify the theoretical framework so that your empirical study helps to develop current theories.

Within many disciplines, some theories are more popular than others. For this reason, some students feel under pressure to include the most popular theories of the time. This approach is seldom successful. Your research questions should determine the relevant theoretical framework. If a theory seems irrelevant to your questions, do not use it.

6.2 Reviewing the literature

A literature review shows that you have done some reading and considered it. The purpose of the review is to explain facts that are unknown to the reader and that are necessary to understand your position. What you are actually doing is justifying your work by defining a space that has been neglected by others, and thereby developing your own position.

When you discuss books, articles, dissertations and research reports the literature must appear to be necessary to understand the field (see Chapter 7 for more information about how to formulate and develop research questions). If the subsequent research appears unrelated to the literature, you have reviewed the wrong type of literature. Keep in mind that the review should function as a relevant context for your thesis and that every part should have something to say about your research topic.

To illustrate, we will take a look at a master's thesis in political science that studied Islamism and gender by analysing one particular political party, the Algerian Islamist Party (Holmsen, 2009). The research questions asked if patriarchy is a basis for Islamist movements or if such movements are changing their perceptions of women. In the literature review, this student reviewed current research on Islamism, women and Islamism, Islam and modernity, and social movement theory. In her account of social movement theory, she emphasized a topic that was related to the research questions, namely movement ideology (ibid.: 16–19). There are several other topics that she could have addressed which are commonly discussed in social movement theory, such as actor motivation and organizational models. Since they were not related to the particular research questions studied here, they were left out of the discussion. The literature review created coherence between the theoretical and the empirical parts.

It is often difficult to distinguish between relevant and irrelevant literature when you begin to write this section. This confusion has to do with the fact that you are at an early stage in the writing process. Include the literature you think is important. As your work develops, so will your understanding of what to include and what to leave out. During the last phase of your work, go back and take out irrelevant sections (see Chapter 11 on editing). This approach means that you will write more than you will actually use. However, this does not necessarily mean that your work is a waste of time. Perhaps you will use the text you took out somewhere else, in an article or a lecture. Remember that it is much easier to write too much than it is to go back later and incorporate new text.

The different sources of research literature should not be given an equal amount of attention in the review. It is common to use less space on scholarly contributions you will not use later, and give more space to that which is important to form your own argumentation. For example, one or two pages should be used for a historical outline of older and inadequate research, whereas 5–10 pages should be allocated for discussion of the research that is important for your study. If the connection between the literature and your argument is not clear, you must let the reader know why you have included this particular literature. Finally, remember to set aside more space when describing an unknown topic than discussing topics that are widely known by most readers.

A common strategy in reviewing research literature is to go from the general to the specific. This is true for the whole thesis, as well as for each section. In every part of the presentation, begin by introducing the most important contributions in the field. In our example, the student began by presenting studies on Islamism in general. Thereafter, she focused on the research that analysed women and Islamism.

Further, concentrate on the main topics in each presentation. We will see how a student introduced a scholar whose work she wanted to discuss (Revheim, 2004). It is common to present academic traditions and positions, as well as other contextual factors that are important for the academic work. This is how this student began her introduction:

> Samuel P. Huntington has a long and impressive academic record ... Today Huntington is the director of the John Olin Institute of Strategic Studies at Harvard (Dalby, ÓTuathail and Routledge, 1998, p. 170). Huntington can be classified as a realist, but many have also labeled him a neoconservative thinker. Huntington has not been confined to academic circles, on the contrary, he has worked closely with different U.S. governmental agencies (Revheim, 2004: 8)

She continued by presenting his major contributions:

> Huntington first published his interpretation of the evolution of world politics after the Cold War in 1993 in an article in the Journal of Foreign Affairs, titled *The Clash of Civilizations?* (Huntington, 1993a) This evoked an enormous response world-wide ... Three years later he elaborated on his ideas in his book, *The Clash of Civilizations and the Remaking of World Order*. He presents here a new paradigm, as a more meaningful and useful instrument for viewing global politics (Huntington, 1996). (ibid.: 9–10)

After the student introduced the main themes in the work of this scholar, she went on to discuss other areas of his work. When you review the research literature, include examples to illustrate. Remember to place the illustrations in connection to the issues you are discussing.

6.3 Critical analysis – questions and critique

After your have given an overview and described the research literature, you must critically analyse it. A critical analysis implies that you have actively analysed and evaluated the information you have gathered on a particular topic, interpreted the relevancy of the sources, and developed the information into one or more arguments which ends in conclusions. Critical analysis is used when you review and discuss the research literature, and it is used when you analyse the data (see section 9.3). You are expected to always do your reading in a critical manner. A literature review consists of more than just a summary or a description of other people's work. It is an analysis in the sense that you are required to extract different forms of information from the literature and assess it by asking questions and critiquing it. You must consider and evaluate the claims made by the theorists. Is the basis for the claims sound? Do they apply to the situations you will be studying? The aim is to assess definitions of the topic, theories and analytical perspectives, assumptions used, methodologies, gaps in empirical work and conclusions.

The first step in critical analysis is to evaluate what you have read by asking questions that raise more complex issues. The next step is to discuss the literature, which we will address in section 6.4. Questions are useful because they generate ideas, explore concepts and feed into your discussion. There are several strategies for examining statements made by other scholars. Below, we will use Barnes' (2005: 37–49) four strategies for examining statements or propositions: setting up comparisons; questioning the truth of a proposition; checking the validity of an argument; and pinpointing generalizations and assumptions.

Setting up comparisons

Ask yourself if you can think of other views than those expressed in the literature you are examining. When you are going to think critically, the idea is to see if you can find a variety of views and compare their strengths and weaknesses.

One way to set up comparisons is to decide if one proposition is more important than another. Here, you compare *the meaning and the significance of the proposition*. A proposition usually consists of three parts: the basic premise, the claims or the implications deriving from the claims and a conclusion. First, ask questions about the basic premise of the proposition. If the premise is false, the whole argument is faulty. Let us take the following proposition as a simple example: 'All middle-class children are more intelligent than working-class children.' By showing that some middle-class children are but many are not, you have critically analysed the claims made in the proposition. Since the claim is based on a generalization ('all middle-class children'), it is relatively easy to refute it. Otherwise, you would have needed to provide evidence, for example in the form of documentation found in previous research. Second, ask questions about possible consequences of a proposition. Which consequences could such a proposition have for the funding of school programmes? Why are these consequences important, and for whom?

A common way to set up comparisons is *by looking for differences over a period of time*. For example, immigration policies are about to change. You can set up comparisons by asking how immigration policies used to be. Ask how they are now, and how they might be in the future. You can also set up a comparison by *changing the context* to see if this changes the content of the proposition. For example, if you are going to interpret a book or an article, does it make a difference if the text is written by a woman, a person who belongs to an ethnic minority, or a male bureaucrat?

It is also common to distinguish between *positive and negative comparisons*. Positive comparisons point to similarities, whereas negative comparisons point to differences. Below we will take a look at how a student uses negative and positive comparisons in the review of the research literature. This example is a thesis in human geography which analyses the use of microcredit as a strategy to reduce poverty in Ghana, especially among youth and women (Siakwah, 2010). In the following, the student begins by contrasting and outlining the differences between the so-called modernization theorists and dependency theorists when it comes to their views on how poverty is created and removed:

> The modernization theorists contend that poverty is internally created in the developing nations and could only be removed through internal strategies by following the development paths of the advanced world (Hirschman 1958, Myrdal 1971, Schultz 1980) ... The dependency theorists, on the other hand, hold the view that poverty is externally created and can only be eradicated if the developed world alters the unfavorable trade relations with the developing countries (Dos Santos 1973, Bauer 1981, Rodney 1972). (Siakwah, 2010: 13)

Here, the negative comparisons between the modernization and the dependency theorists are used to pinpoint their differences. The student continues by setting up positive comparisons between these two 'grand theories'. The purpose is to point out the similar features that these theories share:

> Gardner et al. (1996) have argued that neither of the grand theories has survived intact as a viable paradigm for understanding change and transformation, or processes of poverty and inequality in time and space. It is noted that the arguments of these theories appear abstract, which meant that they might fail to reflect the complexity of real world situation and thus ended up with circular statements

(Seppälä 1998). That means, they might not be ideal in explaining realistically the problems of global processes. (ibid.: 13)

Although these two theories are different, they share certain limitations and weaknesses that this student uses to dismiss both of them.

Setting up negative and positive comparisons is an effective device for finding out as much as possible about a topic. Comparisons can be made of theories, statements, actions, empirical findings, events, public policies and so forth. Questions of 'Why?' and 'How?' can be turned into 'Why not?' and 'How not?'. The more meanings you compare, the more comprehensive and profound your understanding will be.

Questioning the truth of a proposition

Propositions are seldom true or false. Many propositions depend on facts that strengthen or weaken their truth. Ask yourself: *To what extent or under which circumstances* might something be true or false? There are very few propositions that are true in every situation or in all circumstances.

Questioning the truth of a proposition helps to identify the underlying assumptions. These assumptions are usually not expressed explicitly, but they are important in deciding whether a proposition is true or not. You do this by examining the proposition to see if it is *substantiated*. You may ask 'Is this true?', 'Where is the evidence?' or 'What are the implications?'. The following example is taken from a thesis in sociology which explores how Pashtuns in northern Afghanistan, who traditionally had supported the Taliban, coped after the Taliban fell in 2001 (Langslet, 2008). In the following, this student discusses previous research which analyses how migrants made the decision to leave. The research literature distinguishes between migrants who are forced to leave and migrants who voluntarily leave. The student questions the truth of this distinction. She first outlines the two positions in the research literature:

> Forced migration studies often emphasize violence and categorize migration in relation to its degree of 'forcedness', leaving forced migrants with very little choice about their decision to migrate (Lubkemann 2004; Schmeidl 1996). Forced migrants are understood as trying to protect their current livelihood, while voluntary migrants are seen as trying to improve their livelihood. (Langslet, 2008: 13)

Then she questions the truth of the distinction by identifying the underlying assumptions on which it rests:

> This is a rather reductionist way of understanding an actor's response to a crisis situation, as it fails to scrutinize the actors' agency and the social, economic and

cultural factors influencing a decision on whether to stay or leave (Lubkemann 2004). Furthermore, such an understanding fails to account for variations among migrants. (Langslet, 2008: 13)

Here, she shows that the distinction between the two groups of migrants assumes that forced migrants have little agency and that social, economic and cultural factors do not play a role in their decision to leave. She also shows that these assumptions are not substantiated, due to the variety among migrants. Then she presents an alternative proposition, namely that the decision-making process is similar for both groups, which she attempts to substantiate through documentation:

> After all, wartime migrants are no less rational than voluntary migrants, and their ability to make a decision is not eliminated by the cause of their decision. Thus, even though insecurity and violence are essential, other underlying factors of economic and social nature do interact with the political ones (Schmeidl 1996). It is when several of these factors play together that wartime migration is most likely to occur. (ibid.: 13)

By questioning the truth of a proposition and examining it to see if it is substantiated, this student weakened the proposition. As a result, she opened the door to present an alternative proposition, which she supported by presenting documentation.

Another useful way of questioning the truth of a proposition is to ask questions that help you establish its validity. Here, you attempt to find out if a proposition is based on *false assumptions*. For example, if a study uses intelligence tests and concludes that there are different levels of intelligence among various ethnic groups, you will hardly doubt the conclusion that the respondents scored the way they did on the test. However, you will perhaps ask if this is a good measure of intelligence: 'Is this a good test?', 'Why is it a good test?', 'Why is it not a good test?'.

In other instances, you may ask questions to find out if a proposition is resting on an *inadequate basis*. For example, if a survey has a low response rate, the basis to draw conclusions is hardly present. Or if the sample is non-representative, the study does not provide a basis for generalizations.

If you want to examine if a proposition is true, the first step is *to argue that it is false*. Possible questions are: 'What assumptions are implicit in this proposition?', 'Are they acceptable or not?'. The student above used this approach when she argued that forced migration studies rested on 'a rather reductionist way of understanding an actor's response to a crisis situation' (Langslet, 2008: 13). If the assumptions are unacceptable, new questions need to be raised.

Just as propositions can generate questions, questions can be used *to generate propositions*. For example, the question 'Should intolerant and illiberal groups have the right to voice their views in public debates?' can become a controversial proposition by turning the words around: 'Intolerant and illiberal groups should not have the right to voice their views in public debates.' It is easier to discuss a proposition than a question (see section 6.4 below). There are at least four types of questions that are particularly useful in generating propositions (Barnes, 2005: 43–44). They use the words 'must', 'should', 'can't' and 'shouldn't':

What must we do about [e.g. global warming]?

What should we do about ...?

What can't we do about ...?

What shouldn't we do about ...?

Here are some propositions that are generated from these questions. Perhaps you can add more propositions:

'The international community must take responsibility for global warming.'

'Global warming should be fought in each country.'

'Global warming cannot be ignored.'

'Taxes should not be used to fight global warming.'

Checking the validity of an argument

The first question that should be asked is if the argument is *coherent*. An important criteria of good argumentation is that it is consistent and without contradictions.

The second question is if the argument is *valid*. If so, why is it valid? Validity is not dependent on there being truth in the propositions in the argument. Valid arguments can contain true and false propositions. Validity has to do with the logic of the argument, or if the various pieces fit together. If an argument is to be valid, there must be a logical relationship between the proposition and the conclusion in the argument. If you claim that an argument is invalid, it must be because you think that the argument is illogical.

A useful way to analyse an argument is to ask questions about the *premise* on which the argument rests. A premise is a proposition or a statement that is assumed to be true and from which something else can be inferred. If the premise of an argument is unacceptable, the entire argument can be rejected. Since the premise is wrong, the argument that follows bears no significance. Rejecting the premise of an argument is the most common device for discarding it.

You should examine all premises with a certain degree of scepticism. There are several questions that can be asked about a premise. For example, is the premise only based on an assumption or is there evidence that indicates that it is more substantial? Is it based on scientific knowledge? Or is it based on stereotypes? Watch out for sentences such as 'all students ...,' 'all women ...,' and 'all Muslims'. A premise and an argument should be based on scientific knowledge, not stereotypes.

Pinpointing generalizations and assumptions

When reading a text, ask yourself 'What is being *taken for granted* here?'. By asking this question you will be able to pinpoint generalizations and assumptions. Not all generalizations are inaccurate. Some generalizations are summaries of scientific knowledge, such as the statement 'Global warming has harmful effects on the planet'. Assumptions are not necessarily in and of themselves a sign of poor academic argument, unless they are proven to be false. People make assumptions on a daily basis that are based on previous experience.

Within the academic genre of writing, you are encouraged to make *specific* propositions rather than *general* ones. It is difficult to construct a meaningful argument unless you move from the general to the specific. Stereotypes are, for example, based on generalizations. They are so wide that they fit a variety of situations, and data that fail to support them are overlooked. 'Women are less capable leaders than men' is a sweeping generalization. It is based on an assumption that all women are less capable leaders than all men, even when there is plenty of specific evidence to contradict it.

Nevertheless, there are some types of generalizations that are used within the academic genre. If you conducted a study based on a representative sample of women and men leaders, it is possible to make sound generalizations based on the data you collected and analysed. This is not an unsupported generalization because it is based on evidence produced by research and it is situated in a specific context.

These four strategies for examining statements and propositions, setting up comparisons, questioning the truth of a proposition, checking the validity of an argument and pinpointing generalizations and assumptions will help you to clarify your own thinking. By examining statements, you will find arguments that you can use later in the discussion of the research literature.

6.4 Critical analysis – discussing the literature

After your have asked questions and criticized the literature, the next step is to discuss it. A good literature review demonstrates competencies in finding and selecting items or issues that will be discussed in greater detail. The issues included in the discussion must be important for the field of study. By reading the literature you will be able to find them. The issues you select must also be relevant for your research questions. One illustrative example is the above-mentioned thesis which studied the effect of foreign policy questions on American voters in presidential elections between 1992 and 2008 (Lian, 2010). This student included a discussion of values and attitudes, dimensional voting and party identification, which were later used in an electoral model and in the analysis. These discussions became an integrated part of the overall argument and functioned as a thread from start to finish.

Our aim here is to present briefly how an argumentation is constructed (see also Walton 2006: 1–42). It is important not to confuse propositions and arguments. A *proposition* is a sentence that is true or false. An *argument* is a statement that is used to support or weaken a proposition that is questionable, or open to doubt. Arguments are valid or invalid. A proposition is never valid or invalid, but it can be tested to see if it is true or false. This distinction is the basic equipment for thinking and discussing. In a master's thesis, the argumentation will not be confined to a few logical lines. Instead, the writing will contain an overall argumentation that consists of a chain of arguments. Let us see how to construct an argumentation by chaining arguments.

Statements that are used to support the proposition are called *pro arguments*, and statements that are used to question or weaken the proposition are called *counter arguments* (or rebuttals). For example, the statement 'University education is a good thing' is a proposition. The statement 'After one year, most university graduates are employed' is a pro argument because it supports the proposition. The statement, 'Many university graduates have difficulties getting relevant jobs' is a counter argument, because it weakens the proposition.

Some students mistakenly believe that they are discussing the research literature when they are, in fact, only repeating what some scholars have said. For example, the following statement is not a discussion, but a summary of other scholars' views:

> When attempting to explain how fundamentalist political and religious movements grow, some scholars emphasize the importance of political leadership crisis (Kepel 2002), whereas other scholars stress the political opportunities which are available for these movements to act. (Meyer and Staggenborg 1996)

By simply describing what other scholars think and include references to their work, you are still being descriptive.

It is you who must be critical, basing your judgement on the knowledge you have acquired through a balanced reading or your observations. You can use your critical reading of these scholars to construct your own argument. The idea is to formulate a proposition, which is debated by using pro- and counter arguments. For example:

> Fundamentalist political and religious movement growth is the result of various forms of crises. Kepel (2002) shows that during the 1960s and 70s many Arab leaders used socialist ideology to oppress opposition and control the state. It is reasonable to argue that this leadership crisis created a situation which promoted the growth of Islamic fundamentalism. However, by focusing on political opportunities to act, which Meyer and Staggenborg (1996) do in their study of American conservative religious movements and their opponents, it is obvious that mobilization cannot take place unless the state enables challengers to act.

If you have reached a well-founded conclusion which stands in a logical relationship to the argument above, you should add: 'The conclusion is that …'.

As mentioned above, it is easier to discuss a proposition than a question. It is therefore a good idea to rephrase a question into a proposition which is then discussed. A chain of argumentation is made up of smaller specific arguments combined together. The aim is to support or weaken the proposition. It is common to first present one or more arguments that support the proposition (pro arguments), followed by one or more arguments that weaken the proposition (counter arguments). The arguments that directly support or weaken the proposition are called 'arguments of the first order'. These arguments can, in fact, function as propositions that can be supported or weakened by other arguments. The arguments that support or weaken the first order arguments are called 'arguments of the second order'. Again, these arguments can function as propositions that can be supported or weakened by other arguments, called 'arguments of the third order'. In this way, chains of argumentation are made up of smaller arguments that are connected together. The conclusion is reached when there are no more relevant arguments.

We will now see how a student in sociology organizes his argumentation according to this structure. The following example is taken from a thesis which analyses social mobility among Norwegian-born people of immigrant descent (Hermansen, 2009). This student asks if disadvantages experienced by immigrants are transferred to their children, especially when it comes to their occupational position on the labour market. In order to answer this question, he compares Norwegians of immigrant descent with ethnic Norwegians in the same age group and with similar education. In the following, he discusses the importance of social origins. First, the student presents a proposition in the form of a hypothesis:

> It is a viable hypothesis that inequality in labor-market outcomes between second-generation immigrants and native majority individuals is a result of different social, cultural, and economic resources in their families of origin … (Jonsson 2007). (ibid.: 41)

The hypothesis states that Norwegian-born people of immigrant descent will have less prestigious occupations because they come from more disadvantaged family backgrounds than ethnic Norwegians. In the following, he discusses this hypothesis by presenting arguments for and against it. He first presents several pro arguments which support the hypothesis or the proposition. We have selected three pro arguments. They are 'arguments of first order', that is, arguments which directly support or weaken the proposition:

> Individuals of advantaged social backgrounds may draw upon assistance from parents, relatives, and friends in order to get access to occupational positions ... [P]ersons from advantaged social origins may have intimate knowledge of correct ways of self-presentation and conduct in prestigious elite circles ... [I]ndividuals of advantaged social class backgrounds could have higher work aspirations than their peers of less advantaged backgrounds. (ibid.: 41–42)

Here, the student outlines several reasons why the family backgrounds of these two groups will affect their positions on the labour market. These arguments support the proposition that these groups differ due to different social origins. He then presents a counter-argument which weakens the hypothesis above:

> However ... we can derive a reverse argument, i.e. that persons of less advantaged social origins who attain higher-level educational qualifications are positively selected for higher aspirations than their peers of more advantaged social origins ... (e.g., Boudon 1974; Mare 1980; Breen and Goldthorpe 1997). (ibid.: 42)

The student argues that people who come from less advantaged backgrounds and still have attained a higher-level education must have more resources than people from advantaged backgrounds. He uses this argument to weaken the hypothesis which states that social origin matters. This counter-argument is substantiated by two pro arguments. They are 'arguments of the second order', that is, arguments which support the counter-argument:

> Furthermore, following this line of argument, if second-generation immigrants have higher educational aspirations than their social origin peers in the native majority, this immigrant 'drive' could also spill over to their work aspirations and career-orientations. This *could* give them advantages in the process of occupational attainment ... (ibid.: 42)

Here, he argues that the above 'immigrant drive' which led to high educational aspirations could result in stronger career orientations and better positions on the labour market than their peers. These arguments support the counter-argument which attempts to weaken the original hypothesis about the importance of social origin.

This example demonstrates an overall argumentation that consists of a chain of arguments. It is possible to imagine that the student could have included more arguments. Do you have suggestions for arguments that could be used? Finally, the discussion should end in a conclusion. Do you have a suggestion for a concluding sentence?

Many students make the mistake of only including pro arguments when they want to support a proposition. However, it is important to incorporate counter arguments as well. In doing so, you demonstrate your knowledge of the counter arguments and the ability to look at an issue from more than one angle. When you introduce counter arguments, try to weaken them by using arguments of a higher order. By presenting arguments against a counter-argument, the proposition is supported. A discussion of the research literature consists, then, of a chain of argumentation that includes several pro- and counter arguments combined.

6.5 Evaluating arguments

Some arguments are better than others. The quality of an argument is often judged by three criteria: reliability, significance and validity.

Reliability

If the propositions in an argument are incorrect, the argument is not a good argument. We have seen above that propositions can be based on assumptions that were never questioned or opinions unsupported by evidence. A common strategy is to show that the propositions in the argument are correct and therefore reliable, and correspondingly that the propositions in the counter-argument are incorrect or unreliable. Questioning the truth of a proposition is a useful method to formulate arguments for and against the proposition.

Significance

If it does not matter that the proposition in the argument is correct or incorrect, the argument has little significance for the discussion. Many argumentations attempt to show the importance of a specific argument by weakening the counter-argument. The reason is that the weaker the argument, the less significance it has. When you want to demonstrate the weakness of a counter-argument, reduce its importance and show that it is irrelevant for the discussion.

Validity

An argument usually contains several propositions that may individually be true or false. As noted above, if the argument is to be valid, the different propositions must be coherent. Validity is dependent upon the logical consistency between the propositions and the conclusion of the argument. If the propositions are inconsistent and there is a gap in logical coherence, the argument is invalid.

6.6 Summary

1. The purpose of the literature review is to define the space that has been neglected by other scholars.
2. Coherence should be evident in several sections of the thesis:
   - between theory and empirical facts
   - between the research questions and the larger debates in your field
   - between theory and analysis.
3. When you describe and discuss the research literature:
   - include only relevant literature
   - give more space to important literature you will use later and less space on contributions you will not use
   - go from the general to the specific
   - concentrate on the main topics.
4. The first step in critical analysis is to evaluate the research literature by asking questions which raise more complex issues. You question and critique the literature by:
   - setting up positive and negative comparisons
   - questioning the truth of a proposition
   - checking the validity of an argument
   - pinpointing generalizations and assumptions.
5. The next step in critical analysis is to discuss the research literature. An argumentation consists of:
   - a proposition, which is a sentence that is true or false
   - an argument, which is valid or invalid
   - pro arguments, which support the proposition
   - counter arguments, which weaken the proposition.
6. A discussion of the research literature consists of a chain of argumentation that includes several pro- and counter arguments combined.
7. Arguments are judged by three criteria: reliability, significance and validity.

8 Below is a list of suggestions for opening sentences that are useful when you want to change the direction in your writing (see Barnes, 2005: 144):

   - Previous research offers us a number of examples …
   - What can be said immediately is …
   - This clash of views calls into question …
   - It would hardly be an exaggeration to say that …
   - The problem can be summarized …
   - This problem can be seen from another angle …
   - Is this really a sound reason for saying …?
   - A second argument which cannot be ignored is …
   - We must allow for …
   - From this, it would seem that not all …
   - This explains why …
   - Alternatively, … in addition … by contrast …
   - One of the most obvious examples …
   - A similar topic is taken up by … who says that …

6.7 Action plan

1 Write a critical analysis of two books that are relevant for your topic.
2 First review the literature by describing it.
3 Then, critically consider and evaluate the claims made by the authors. Ask yourself:

   - What is the basic premise of the claims?
   - Is the basic premise sound? For example, is it believable? Where is the evidence?
   - What are the consequences derived from the claims made?
   - Do the authors make generalizations?

4 The next step in critical analysis is to discuss the research literature:

   - select one issue and formulate a proposition which can be discussed
   - formulate two pro arguments and two counter arguments
   - formulate arguments of the second and the third order to each of the arguments above. Can you think of more relevant arguments that need be included?
   - try to weaken the counter arguments by using counter arguments of a higher order
   - formulate a conclusion to the discussion.

7
How do I formulate research questions?

Many students find that formulating research questions is one of the most challenging aspects of writing a master's thesis. Have you ever had someone ask you what your research questions are, only to hear yourself mumble 'I'm working on it'? Students often struggle with solving the puzzle of what a scientific question is. From the perspective of the student, as well as more experienced scientists, posing research questions can imply a certain level of frustration.

It is a problem in many master's theses that the questions are vague. This does not mean that the questions are uninteresting. Vague questions often indicate that you lack clarity as to what the problems are which you are going to solve. In some cases, the result will be that you collect too much data or collect the wrong type of data. The lack of specified research questions also creates problems when you are getting ready to analyse the data. What type of answers can you possibly be looking for when you are not sure which questions you have? Finally, if you do not have specified questions, you will not know when your work is finished. The benefit of having specified research questions is that you know that your analysis is finished when all the questions are answered.

One would think that it is fairly easy to pose a scientific question. Yet, most students as well as scientists think that it is often more difficult to find and formulate good questions than to find the answers. Although formulating research questions is difficult, it is not a mystery that cannot be solved. In the social sciences, questions are of a particular kind. They are constructed in a certain way that is common for most social science research, and our aim in this chapter is to show you how. We are unable to offer a universal recipe for formulating scientific questions, but perhaps we can give you a general idea and point out some principal ingredients in a scientific question in the social sciences. Hopefully, this will help you to formulate more complete research questions.

According to American sociologist Robert Merton (1965), the questions that matter in the social sciences are 'questions so formulated that the answers to them will confirm, amplify, or variously revise some part of what is currently taken as knowledge in the field' (1965: x). Merton attempts to identify the principal ingredients in scientific questions in sociology and in social scientific enquiry generally, and he outlines three principal components (1965: xii–xiii). First is the origination question, or what we here call the *overall question*, a statement of what you want to know. Second is the *rationale*, stating why you want to have the particular questions answered. Third are the *specified questions* that point towards possible answers to the overall question in terms that satisfy the rationale for having raised it. Most students succeed in posing overall questions. However, many stop here and fail to include the other two components. Later, we will organize the discussion according to Merton's distinctions. Before we do so, we want to give a brief outline of research questions in quantitative and qualitative studies.

7.1 Research questions in quantitative and qualitative theses

When students begin to develop a topic for a thesis and formulate research questions, they will find that the amount of information about different topics varies greatly (see section 1.2). In some cases, a lot of research has been conducted, which students can access and use to formulate research questions. In other cases, there is little research and information available. Often the type of research questions students will be able to pose varies according to the amount of information that is available before they begin their study.

When few studies have been conducted and you only have vague perceptions of what you are going to study, it is difficult to formulate very specific research questions. In this situation, the research questions often centre on a *topic* in the sense that you describe the topic and specify what you want to know about it. This type of question is usually broad and open. This approach is sometimes used in *qualitative studies*. One example is an ethnographic study of the use of electric vehicles in the UK (Brady, 2010). Although some studies had been conducted in this area, they were small and limited. This student defined a topic, namely 'Electric car culture', which she wanted to study. She used ethnography to document patterns of use and driving styles, and the values of the drivers. We have previously described how you find a topic for your thesis (Chapter 1), and there is a rather fluid boundary between developing a topic and posing research questions. As we pointed out in Chapter 1, a topic must be defined and developed.

A description of a topic can provide the basis for *asking more limited questions*. Often you will have some information about the topic. If this is the case, you can ask factual questions and use the thesis to answer them. This approach is used in *quantitative* as well as qualitative studies. One example of a qualitative study is a thesis in sociology where the student asked if the central government policies on health and education in the UK changed much after Tony Blair's New Labour governments of 1997–2007 took over from Margaret Thatcher's Conservative governments of 1979–97. He answered this question by conducting a qualitative analysis of government documents (Holland, 2009). Another example is a thesis in education which asked about the effects of planned change on organizational culture in a large college in the UK. This student used quantitative and qualitative data to answer this question (Stakes, 2010). Indeed, the focus of this chapter is how to formulate these types of research questions.

Finally, in some situations the topic is so researched beforehand that the research questions are formulated as one or more *hypotheses* and the purpose of the study is add more information or revise previous knowledge. In order to test hypotheses, there is usually a need to conduct a *quantitative* study. An example of this approach is found in a thesis in political science which studies the role of foreign policy in American presidential elections (Lian, 2010). As we will see below, this student begins by posing an overall question. After he has reviewed the relevant research and theory in the field, he creates a voting model and generates several hypotheses, which he tests by doing a quantitative analysis of election surveys. The limitation of this approach is that the thesis is directed only at falsifying the hypotheses, which might mean that the student has overlooked important new and unexpected information.

As we see, research questions in qualitative studies tend to differ from those in quantitative studies as it relates to scope and degree of specificity. This might lead some students who plan to conduct a qualitative study to mistakenly assume that they do not have to put much effort into formulating research questions. The same is often true for students who write theoretical theses. They tend to present vague research questions in the introduction (which they should; see section 10.1), but these questions are not developed further in the thesis. The result is that the reader does not really understand what the student wants to do. In some cases, the student also operates with more specified research questions which are scattered throughout the thesis.

In some books on qualitative research methods, authors claim that you should wait to formulate research questions until you have begun the data collection. This approach tends to create a number of problems for students. They risk collecting either too much or sometimes irrelevant data, which means extra work and is a waste of time. Qualitative data are often more difficult to handle than quantitative data. Therefore, studies based on qualitative data demand as much planning when it comes to formulating research questions as quantitative studies do.

This does not mean that research questions cannot be adjusted once the data collection has begun. Adjusting research questions, methods and analysis is a process that takes place continually throughout your work on the thesis. However, it is easier to adjust research questions after the data collection has begun than it is to formulate completely new questions that must fit data which are already collected. The same is true for theoretical theses, which require research questions to be precise. Vague questions tend to result in incoherent discussions.

7.2 Overall research questions

When you are going to formulate research questions, you must first present one or more overall questions, meaning a statement of what you want to know (see sections 1.1–1.2). This sentence can be relatively wide and inclusive. At this stage, think of a problem that stimulates your curiosity. Is there something you do not understand or something you don't know? The question should be of general interest. Why is something this way and not another way?

Your ability to pose research questions is related to your knowledge of the field. If you have little knowledge about a topic, you will not ask good questions. This is the reason behind our advice that once you have selected a topic, the next step is to study, review and discuss the research literature (see Chapter 6). Use the knowledge you obtained through your reading to write down possible questions.

When you are posing questions within the social sciences, look for the actors (i.e. the acting units). This means that the actions which are analysed must be specific. They cannot be 'the society', 'the norms', 'the culture' and so forth. Even if the topic of the thesis is 'a local community', for example, remember the simple fact that people act and not the local community as such. The actors must be identified in the overall questions, and so must their actions (i.e. a reference to specific actors in specific groups or societies).

Different types of overall questions

There are several different types of overall questions (Merton, 1965: xiii–xix). Whereas some questions are wide, other questions are more limited in scope. Questions vary also according to the type of knowledge that is sought.

One important type of question calls for *discovering facts*. It may be needless to say that before facts can be explained, they must be established. Everyday knowledge is sometimes based on assumptions instead of facts, and one aim in research is to discover a particular body of facts. It would be premature to ask 'why' or to try to explain something before the facts are ascertained. For example, if you want to explain why ethnic minority status has effects on positions in the labour market you must first demonstrate that there are differences in occupational status between the ethnic majority and minority populations. The following example is taken from the thesis in sociology which studied social mobility among Norwegians of immigrant descent (Hermansen, 2009). The student compared occupational positions between this group and ethnic Norwegians in the same age group and with similar education. He asked the following descriptive question:

> Do second-generation immigrants gain access to advantaged positions in the social structure on par with their native majority peers? (ibid.: 2)

This question was directed at finding facts about the occupational positions of the two groups. Some students use their theses to merely find and present facts. These types of master's theses are usually boring. Although posing descriptive questions and finding facts are important, this is only one element in developing a research question.

Descriptive questions are only one of a variety of overall questions. Another type focuses on the search for uniformities of relations between classes of phenomena. One example is: 'How may society be multicultural and yet maintain social cohesion?' Another example is: 'Which factors in a given country affect the crime rates in that country?' These types of overall questions call for more than merely establishing facts. They ask *why* an observed state of affairs exists. The concern here is to explain a phenomenon, to seek reasons and causes. For example, the student who studied American presidential elections asked:

> How important are opinions on foreign policy values and issues for American voters when determining their final vote in the general elections? (Lian, 2010: 8)

This student attempts to find out the effect that policy preferences have on voting behaviour. He does so by suggesting a relationship between two classes of variables, namely opinions on foreign policy values and voting in general elections. The question suggests *classes* of variables that could be taken into account but do not yet suggest the *particular* variables in each class to be considered. As stated above, there are different types of overall questions. At this stage, it is common to play with several. Asking different types of overall questions is an important stage in the process of formulating specified research questions.

A large number of overall questions within the social sciences address the relations between variables within one or more societal *institutions*. Examples of questions focusing on the institutional sphere of society are studies on the educational institution, the legal institution, the religious institution, politics and so forth. We will illustrate these types of questions by taking a look at a master's thesis in education, where the student analysed the consequences of decentralizing educational systems in Australia, Canada, Finland, Norway and Sweden. The two main overall questions were:

> Does the transition of educational authority from central to local level affect student achievement? Does a potential relationship between local autonomy and student achievement still exist after controlling for socio-economic status and immigrant background? (Haug, 2009: 3–4)

In this case, the questions are restricted to a particular institutional sphere, namely the educational systems where decentralization reforms have been implemented. These types of question have a double objective. On the one hand, they direct the attention towards that which is distinctive to that particular institution, which here is a particular type of educational system. On the other hand, the questions can be extended to wider classes of situations or institutions. It is easy to see how the questions above with little revision can be addressed to other institutional spheres, such as health care or the political sphere, where the aim is to study consequences of implemented reforms.

Some overall questions focus on the *application of particular concepts*. A popular topic since the 1990s is identity. There is a wide variety of identities that can be studied – national, ethnic, religious, cultural, social class, gender and sexual – and there is a wide variety of approaches that can be applied. Whereas some attempt to define and outline the construction of specific identities, others use the concept to explain variations in the behaviour of people and the consequences this behaviour has for society.

Another type of overall question is to *clarify concepts or ideas* that no longer seem to be adequate. One example is the question of whether theories of modernity are adequate to describe contemporary Western societies or if one must use concepts of post-modernity, late modernity or even post-secularity.

It is also possible to distinguish between overall questions which centre on *processes* and those which centre on *patterns*. Overall questions which focus on processes are looking at events or factors that take place over a longer period of time (diachronic). One illustrative example is the above-mentioned thesis which analysed American elections (Lian, 2010). The first overall question is followed by a second question, which includes a time factor and points to processes that have taken place over time. The two overall questions are:

> [1] How important are opinions on foreign policy values and issues for American voters when determining their final vote in the general elections?
>
> [2] How has this changed over time in the period between 1992 and 2008? (ibid.: 8)

Overall questions which focus on patterns are looking at factors that take place at a specific moment in time (synchronic). One example is a study which attempted to analyse the reasons for the 2003 American invasion of Iraq (Lindviksmoen, 2007). This thesis was limited to one event that took place at one specific moment.

Contrasts and differences

When you are going to pose an overall question, it is important to emphasize *contrasts*. We have previously mentioned that a thesis which only establishes something as a fact is relatively uninteresting. A thesis is more interesting when there is an attempt to explain the established facts. In an explanation, it is not enough to ascertain that something is a fact, you must also ascertain that something else is *not* a fact. Ask: 'Why does this phenomenon appear in this particular way and not in other ways?'

A useful way to find explanations is to direct the questions towards differences. For example, differences can be found between two points of *time*. One example is the above-mentioned study of American voter opinions and behaviours between 1992 and 2008 (Lian, 2010). Another type of contrast can be between two or more *groups*. One example of this type of question is a thesis in psychology which studied the organization of treatment, care and support for HIV-positive people in rural South Africa by comparing different formal and informal organizations (Vaage, 2010). Differences can also be found in understandings of *concepts, theories* and *discourses*. One example is a thesis in sociology which compared theories on the body in the work of Foucault and symbolic interactionism (Hestad, 2008). Another example is a student in human geography who examined different forms of discourses about rape in American newspaper media in 2006 (Bitsch, 2010).

It is also possible to focus on differences between *theoretical assumptions and observed facts*. An example is a thesis which focused on theories about globalization and the role of the state in the economy (Vold, 2007). While some theories argue that the world economy is so globalized that the nation state is no longer relevant, others claim that the world economy is no more international than it was before the First World War. In much of the literature, transnational companies are seen as the principal actors. This student compared these theories with data from Venezuela and analysed the role of the state in turning the Venezuelan petroleum industry into a tool for development. In this way, he was able to discuss the differences between theoretical claims and empirical data. Finally, it is possible to combine a set of contrasts in the same overall question.

Overall questions can be constructed in various ways, and in more ways than we have mentioned here. These questions are of different kinds and they have different sources. Whereas some questions centre on facts, others are directed towards the adequacy of concepts, theories and ideas. Some deal with the causes of specific phenomena, and others are concerned with their consequences. The important issue is that asking overall questions is not the same as formulating complete research questions. It is only the first ingredient.

7.3 The rationale of the questions

The next step in the formulation of a research question is the rationale or the justification of the question (Merton, 1965: xix–xxvi). Why are you asking this question? Why is it worth your time and effort? You must state what your reasons are for why this question deserves the attention of the reader as well as yourself. The rationale specifies how other parts of science or social practices will benefit from answering the question.

Theoretical rationale

The most important rationale for an overall question is its interest for the scientific community. Merton (1965: xix) distinguishes between *scientifically trivial* and *scientifically consequential* questions. If the question and its answer are going to be consequential for science, they must be relevant for other ideas and observations in the field. This means that it is not enough that you think your question is interesting. Historically, science has been justified by curiosity (i.e. that knowledge is a self-contained end). But if you want your research to be more than a hobby, you must show that it will extend knowledge in one way or another. Because science is a collective project, your research must be relevant for other theories and studies in the field.

Social science research has often been justified by a double relevance. This means that the same research has importance for systematic knowledge as well as practical use. Social scientists disagree whether their research must have both a practical rationale and a theoretical rationale, and the balance between the two. We will not get into this debate here. Our claim is that all overall questions must have a theoretical rationale. In some cases, overall questions will also have a practical rationale. We will describe both types below and attempt to point out the cases where the practical rationale is relevant.

The *theoretical rationale* claims that a question is worth asking because its answers will expand systematic knowledge. This rationale takes various forms. First, an overall question can be justified by stating that existing theory is useful to understand certain phenomena which have not been examined before in terms of this theory. One example is to use contemporary theories of social movements to analyse historic political movements. The purpose of this approach is to detect aspects of these movements that have been ignored by older research. Second, a question can be justified by pointing out perceived inconsistencies in previous research and suggesting that they can be reconciled by demonstrating that the inconsistencies are apparent rather than real. The third theoretical rationale points out gaps in current theories or knowledge. In the thesis on social mobility mentioned above, the student presented a similar rationale. He argued that his study would contribute with important new knowledge in the field, since there was a gap in current research (Hermansen, 2009: 2–3, 25).

Practical rationale

The other type of rationale discussed here is a *practical rationale*. A practical rationale states that a question is worth posing because its answer will have practical consequences for a social group or for society. Many master's theses in the social sciences justify the overall questions by claiming that the answers to these questions will improve the situation of disadvantaged groups or help society deal with conflicts or pressing social issues. One example is a thesis in psychology where two students analysed different treatments of adolescents engaging in non-suicidal self-injury (Lie and Bø, 2010). Several theses in psychology which aim at improving the treatment of various forms of mental disorders and illnesses will tend to have a practical rationale in addition to a theoretical one.

A practical rationale can also be based on the fact that new developments in society are taking place. The purpose of the research is, then, to contribute to new knowledge and understanding. For example, the increasing number of Muslims in Western countries has led to a growing interest in the study of Islam and other religions, as well as the study of ethnic and religious minorities. The interest in research based on a practical rationale tends to increase when social changes are defined as social problems leading to social conflicts. For example, American social science has long traditions of doing research on discrimination and racism.

European social scientists did not demonstrate much interest in these topics until the 1960s and 1970s when racial and ethnic minorities became of a noteworthy size. Historic and social changes affect the types of questions scientists are asking and the reasons why they are asking them.

7.4 Specified questions

We have seen that overall questions differ in scope as well as in the degree of specificity. There is, therefore, a need for specifying the overall questions further. They must be rephrased into one or more questions which will indicate the observations that will give an answer to each overall question. Only then have the research questions definitively been posed (Merton, 1965: xxvi). An example is the following overall question: 'What is the relationship between religion and violence?' This is a question about the connections between two phenomena without any indication about the observations that are required to give an answer to it. It can be rephrased into the following specified question: 'Are there elements in the ideologies of Christianity and Islam that justify the use of violence?' The question is now specified in a way that it indicates the variables that must be studied to give an answer to it, namely the ideological elements of Christianity and Islam.

It is important to be aware that one overall question often has to be recast into several specified questions. If we take a look at the overall question above, we can think of many specified questions that can be asked: 'Do religious people favour the use of violence more than non-religious people do? Do religious people engage more in violent acts than non-religious people do? Do all religious organizations promote the use of violence? If not, which organizations promote the use of violence? Which organizations speak against the use of violence?' We could go on. As you see, these specified questions go in very different directions. Some imply the study of people's attitudes, whereas other questions imply the study of people's actions, religious ideologies or religious organizations. Unless the overall question is specified, you will not really know what kind of observations (study of people's attitudes, people's actions, religious texts, religious leaders or religious organizations) you should be doing.

In most instances, you must answer a number of specified questions in order to answer the overall question. We will use Hermansen's thesis (2009) to illustrate. As mentioned before, his overall question is:

> The general question explored in this study is: Do second-generation immigrants gain access to advantaged positions in the social structure on par with their native majority peers? (Hermansen, 2009: 2)

In order to answer this question, this student had to find various aspects of second-generation immigrants which could possibly affect their positions in the social structure. For example, he studied their social origin and their educational qualifications. He also had to clarify what he meant by 'positions in the social structure', which he defined as positions on the labour market. The student recast his overall question into several specified questions, of which we will mention two:

> [1] Do second-generation immigrants experience equal access to employment relative to native majority peers with similar educational qualifications and social origins?
>
> [2] If employed, do second-generation immigrants experience equal access to different occupational class positions relative to native majority peers with similar educational qualifications and social origins? (Hermansen, 2009: 7–8, 73, 87)

Here, he explores whether the people he studies experience equal opportunities. He first asks if individuals gain access to employment and then if they gain access to specific occupational positions. When the overall question has been rephrased to a number of specified questions, as illustrated here, the research questions have been definitely posed.

When you are going to specify the research questions, do so by writing an introduction to the questions. Use the research literature to frame the questions and justify their relevance. The example below is taken from a master's thesis in psychology mentioned above which studied the organization of treatment, care and support for HIV-positive people in rural South Africa (Vaage, 2010). Notice how the student justifies the overall question by claiming that it is relevant due to the gap in previous research:

> Though many health scientists have drawn attention to the role of social capital as a way to illuminate the quality of healthcare in communities there is yet little current research on the topic (Campell, 2005). This thesis investigates the role of social capital in promoting treatment, care, and support for HIV/AIDS affected people in a poor marginalized community by examining the levels of participation and cooperation between formal and informal healthcare structures in the community. (Vaage, 2010: 18)

Once this question is presented, the student uses the research literature to give a deeper understanding of the question:

> In accordance with Derose and Varda's (2009) and Foley and Edward's (1999) recommendations for the use of social capital in academic research the thesis will not focus on cognitive dimensions of social capital but on structural aspects. (ibid.: 18)

We understand that there are two dimensions often studied by scholars who use the particular type of theory mentioned here, and that this student chooses to use one dimension. After he has specified why he wants to focus on one dimension, he recasts the overall question into four specified questions:

[1] In which ways do formal and informal organizations provide treatment, care and support to HIV positive people in the village?

[2] How do the organizations cooperate and coordinate their work?

[3] To what degree do organizations working in the community cooperate and communicate with formal structures of the government?

[4] What are the main constraints for providing efficient treatment, care and support for HIV positive people in the village? (Vaage, 2010: 18–19)

This student could have described and discussed each question even further than what was done here. A list of specified research questions easily bores the reader. A useful way to deepen the understanding of each question is to pose additional questions that indicate possible answers. If we take a look at the third question above, we will see that the student could have developed it further. For example, he could have added questions such as: 'Do they have formal agreements with the government? If so, which parts of the government?' He could also have turned the question upside down and imagined the opposite answers by asking: 'Or do they only have informal cooperation with governmental agencies?' Can you think of other questions that could have been added?

By using the research literature to present the overall and the specified questions, you give the reader a more thorough understanding of the questions you are asking. You also create expectations by turning the questions upside down. Framing the questions this way also gives coherence between your discussion of the literature and the research you are about to do.

7.5 Adjustments during the research process

Formulating and specifying the research questions take place throughout the entire process of writing a thesis. Once you have found a topic, it is a good idea to write down a number of possible questions. When you read the literature, you will recast the questions as a result of more knowledge. During the search for a research design and method (see Chapter 8), your questions will perhaps change again. Sometimes, you will discover that it is very difficult, if not impossible, to find empirical material that can be used. In other cases, you will realize that your questions are so broad that the effort of trying to answer them will take too much time. Some students find that the data do not provide answers to their questions, or that the data shed light on questions not posed. In both cases, the questions need to be revised. In the first case, old questions must be excluded. In the second, new questions must be incorporated. The process of reformulating questions is common, which means that the process of formulating research questions is not really finished until the analysis is done. However, what we are discussing here are minor adjustments. Do not let this lead you to believe that you can skip the difficult work of formulating research questions. If you do, your whole work will be affected by it.

7.6 Summary

1. Formulating research questions is one of the most challenging aspects of writing a thesis.
2. It is a problem in many theses that the research questions are vague and underdeveloped.
3. The type of research questions often varies according to the amount of information that is available.
4. Research questions in qualitative and quantitative studies vary in scope and specificity.
5. The three principal ingredients of research questions are:
   - overall questions
   - rationale of the questions
   - specified questions.
6. The research questions are often adjusted during the entire thesis process.

7.7 Action plan

1. Formulate one overall question relating to the topic you have selected for your thesis.
2. Give a rationale for the question. What is the theoretical rationale? Should you include a practical rationale?
3. Formulate three specified questions to the overall question. Use the research literature when doing so.
4. Discuss the questions with your advisor, fellow students and other relevant discussion partners.

8
Easier said than done – choosing a suitable research design and method

The starting point of research is usually finding and formulating a topic. When you begin looking at designing your research project, considerations of methodological issues become part of this process. As noted in Chapter 7, searching for a method sometimes leads to further specifications or revisions of your research questions. In fact, formulating research questions and finding the proper method(s) often take place at the same time. It is a good idea to begin thinking about methodological issues as soon as possible. Whether you have a qualitative or a quantitative study in mind, preparations must be made beforehand. There are several choices involved in conducting research, such as methodological traditions and approaches, choosing a methodological strategy that takes the constraints on your time and money into consideration, ethical issues relevant to your research idea, and finding data that are available, reliable and valid. The focus of this chapter is to look at important issues you must consider to design a coherent research project.

This chapter is not about various research methods. Our aim here is to point out some of the issues you need to address when designing your research. In the social sciences, different methodological assumptions and beliefs are widely debated, which have consequences for methodological approaches and choices (see, for example, Hart, 2008a: 193–276). There are many excellent books and other sources dedicated to research methods in the social sciences. We want to mention two book series that offer brief guidance to different methods (see section 5.7). Sage's *Little Green Books* series teaches quantitative methods in the social sciences, and Sage's *Little Blue Books* series covers qualitative methods. Also, take a look at *Sage Research Methods Online*, which is a tool to help students (http://srmo.sagepub.com). Our advice is that you study the literature relevant for your field and your thesis. Ask your tutor or advisor to help you.

8.1 What is a research method?

A master's thesis must set aside a chapter or a section to describe the steps that will be undertaken to address the research questions. Usually, the methods section follows the formulation of the research questions. Whether you use quantitative or qualitative methods, or whether the data consist of surveys, interviews, observations, documents or texts, you must describe the considerations that led you from the research questions to the applicable method by which those questions may be studied. This means that a coherent research design has a logical relationship between the research questions and the method.

There is 'an arsenal' of different research methods. Every research method has its advantages and disadvantages. There are always other ways to do research and answer the research questions you have posed. Here, we will view research methods as different tools in the research toolbox. It is a strategy or a technique you use to solve problems and acquire new knowledge. The main question is: What do you have to do to acquire the necessary knowledge to answer your research questions?

It is important to remember that all research takes place within paradigms and models that are considered acceptable within various fields of study. Each research method rests on assumptions of truth and perceptions of what the world is like (Crotty, 1998). There is an ongoing debate on qualitative and quantitative methods in the social sciences, a debate that raises issues of what science is, the nature of knowledge and values in research. This debate was previously characterized by deep antagonism. Now there is an acknowledgement that both methods have strengths and weaknesses.

Our approach is that one method cannot, in principle, be considered better or worse than the other. The most important aspect of a method is whether or not it helps you to answer your research questions. This means that you must find the best tools to serve this purpose. Another important issue that must be considered relates to ethical dimensions of the method in question (see section 8.3).

It is a good idea to be open to various research methods. Look to see if different methods can be combined rather than locking yourself into considering only one method (Creswell, 2008). Many scientists have found that it is often fruitful to mix different methods (Teddlie and Tashakkori, 2008). At the same time, you must consider how extensive your research should be in the time you have available. Do not make your thesis too complicated by employing several research methods. If you want to mix methods, a good strategy is to focus on one method, which is supplemented by other methods. For example, the starting point of a thesis can be a summary of findings from existing surveys, which are studied in more detail by a qualitative study. These matters should be discussed with your advisor.

8.2 Useful strategies for designing a master's thesis

Master's-level students face a number of constraints and dilemmas. First of all, most students have limited time available. Then there is the economic limitation, which means that one cannot afford costly data collection. At the same time, it is in the interest of every student to plan a project that provides as much information as possible. The challenge is to design a research project that can be completed within these constraints. Here we will outline good strategies commonly used to design master's theses. It is important to remember that these strategies are not mutually exclusive, but can be combined. There are also more strategies than those mentioned here.

Fill gaps in previous research

As you study previous research, you will sometimes find that the scope of the research is limited. The purpose of the new research is to fill gaps in previous research. An illustrative example is feminist research, which often has collected a lot of new information that male scientists have overlooked. By studying topics male scientists have ignored, they have uncovered large areas of society that otherwise had remained in the dark. One master's thesis within this genre was conducted by a student in history who studied two child emigration societies based in Birmingham and Manchester between 1870 and 1914 (Ward, 2010). Although there had been a scholarly interest in child emigration to Australia, this topic has largely been ignored in previous research when it came to children taken to Canada.

If you want to use this strategy, one possible idea is to use data from one of the many surveys that have been conducted and formulate new research questions that scientists have ignored. These questions can be answered by analysing the quantitative data in a different way than previously done, and perhaps by collecting new qualitative data. A student used a similar approach when she wanted to study segmented assimilation among Arab Americans in the Detroit Metro area (Weaver, 2010). She used previous census data and collected new interview data from Arab Americans living in the Detroit Metro area. Another idea is to use the many suggestions for further research that usually come at the end of scholarly articles and books to pose your own research questions. Several of the completed master's theses that are used as examples in this book have the aim of filling gaps in previous research.

Reappraise previous research

In some cases, the problem with previous research is not that its scope is limited, but that it is based on mistakes and misinterpretations. Therefore, a common strategy is to reappraise previous research by using new interpretive tools, perspectives or methods. A shift in point of view can fundamentally affect the research conducted. One example of this approach is to re-analyse data collected at a specific point in time. The aim is to see if new information is found by using different theories, explanatory strategies or analytical tools than those used earlier. One example is African American historical research. In American research, Euro-American perspectives were taken as the norm and African American experiences and perspectives were largely ignored. By using different analytical perspectives, frames of reference and methods, African American scientists found a vast amount of information that Euro-American scientists had misinterpreted.

Repeat previous research

The strategy here is to attempt to repeat previous research either in another context or at another time. Let us first take a look at repeating research *in another context*. For example, a student finds information about research conducted in a specific context and decides to conduct similar research in a different context. One example of this approach is found in a study of Islamism and gender (Holmsen, 2009). These topics have been studied in several contexts, but this student decided to focus on a specific Algerian political party. A similar approach is taken when one repeats research *at another time*. It is possible to look at studies conducted a few years ago and repeat the same study today. The purpose is to detect possible changes that have taken place between the two points in time.

Case studies

This strategy opens up for the study of one case or the comparison of two or more cases. The characteristic feature of a case study is that the findings from the study apply solely to this case and cannot be generalized to other populations. Case studies seem to be a useful strategy for many master's-level students. The reason is that a case is relatively limited, which makes it useful for small research projects. One example is a thesis in social anthropology where the student studied local Liverpool fans' experience of commercial changes in British football (Gustavsen, 2010). Another example is a student in education who evaluated the effects of planned change in organizational culture among staff who presented higher education programmes in a large college in the UK (Stakes, 2010). While these students analysed one case, other students prefer to compare two or more cases. For example, a law student compared two cases in her thesis, namely affirmative action in the US and the UK (Herron, 2010). Another example is a student in sociology who compared the social policy with special reference to health and education during the Conservative governments of Margaret Thatcher (1979–97) and the New Labour governments of Tony Blair (1997–2007) (Holland, 2009). Finally, a student in political science compared five cases in his thesis, namely five American presidential elections (Lian, 2010). These cases are limited to defined theories that are voiced, or actions that took place, in a given context at a specific point in time.

Write a thesis within the frames of a research programme

Many master's-level students prefer to conduct an independent study. Other students choose to write a thesis within a large research programme directed by a professor at their university or college. Although the latter strategy often implies certain limitations regarding research topic and methods, it has several benefits. You will be part of a large group of scientists who will take an interest in your work. You will learn about research by interacting with the researchers and the other students in the programme. You will also extend your academic network, which can be helpful in pursuing an academic career (see Chapter 4).

8.3 Practical and ethical considerations when collecting data

Whichever strategy you choose, all research needs data. Data can be whatever is deemed necessary to answer your research questions. The data may take the form of survey data, interview data or observations. Or the data may take the form of texts, such as academic books, public reports, historic documents, photography, film and so on.

It is common to distinguish between *primary* and *secondary data*. Primary data are first-hand accounts produced at the time of the event. Survey data and interview data are some examples of primary data. So are historic records and documents, speeches and government documents. These may be available in their original form or they may be reproduced in a book or on the Internet. An important feature of primary data is that they have not been interpreted by others. This does not mean that primary data are objective. Surveys and interview data can be coloured by the researchers who formulated the questions and collected the data. The authors who produce the first-hand accounts interpret situations, problems, actions and objects, and their interpretations are also coloured by their contexts. In contrast, secondary data interpret and analyse primary sources, which means that they are somewhat removed from the event itself. Secondary data consist of critique, commentaries, analyses and informed views, often found in books, newspapers and other forms of publications.

Another important distinction is that between *data* and *evidence* (Barnes, 2005: 160–161). Primary and secondary data are not in themselves evidence used to support arguments. A student who uses primary or secondary data (e.g. survey data or government documents) will not argue that the data in and of themselves are the evidence, but rather that the evidence can be found in these data. Data must be questioned and analysed before they can be used as evidence. This is why data, such as interview data, survey data, research literature or historic records, must be evaluated and discussed rather than used without analysis or criticism.

This brings us to different ways by which you can *evaluate* data. Once you have identified possible data, you must make sure you find the data you need. You must also consider how the data can be collected, in sufficient quantity and of the necessary quality. Below, we will outline some criteria commonly used to evaluate data.

Sample

All research uses some form of procedure to select the data that are going to be included in the study. Not all research requires, however, the careful sampling needed when the population is too large for all units to be studied, for example in statistical surveys. The size of the sample is dependent upon the type of research you are going to do. As a master's student, it is important to carefully consider the size of the sample with your limited time and money in mind.

Considering sample size is relevant for all students who are writing a master's thesis. If you are going to analyse texts, you will have to make a selection of sources. The available literature is extensive within most fields and it is not likely that you will be able to include everything. What are the most important contributions? What is considered to be a 'must'? Which criteria should you use to select what to include and what to leave out? Discuss these issues with your advisor.

A sample in empirical studies refers to both units of analysis and variables selected for the study. The size of the sample differs drastically in quantitative and qualitative studies. In quantitative studies, there are minimum requirements for the size of the sample in order to make the study reliable. If you are planning to conduct a quantitative study, use one of the numerous excellent textbooks on statistics that are available. If you are planning to conduct a qualitative study, check with your advisor about the size of the sample. Master theses based on qualitative studies vary in this area. To illustrate, a thesis in sociology can be based on nine interviews (Susaas, 2010) or 34 interviews (Gustavsen, 2011). In addition, discuss with your advisor the number of variables that should be included.

It is not necessary to include all the relevant information regarding the research questions, as long as you explain to the reader what you exclude and why. Common explanations are that you did not have time to collect all the available data and that it would cost too much to do so. The amount of data can quickly become unmanageable. If you collect too much data, you will find that the sheer amount becomes difficult to handle and you end up wasting time on reducing it to a workable size. So plan data collection carefully.

Availability

Before data collection begins, check to see if the data will be available. Is the literature available at the library or online? If you want to conduct an empirical study, will you be able to access the data you need? Do the data already exist or do you have to collect them? If you want to interview individuals, what is the likelihood that they will want to cooperate with you? Will you be able to access the group you want to study? These questions need be answered as quickly as possible. There are examples of students who planned a study carefully, only to find that they were unable to access the informants. It takes a lot to recover from such a setback and get started with a new study.

Reliability

Another issue that must be considered is the quality of data. The word 'reliability' is often associated with measurements in quantitative studies, but reliability also has to do with the thoroughness with which data has been collected. Reliable data are data that can be trusted. In some instances, reliability is connected to the trustworthiness of primary and secondary sources, such as books, documents and research reports. In other instances, the reliability of data is found by repeating the observations, tests or questions to see if independent measurements of one and the same phenomenon produce consistent results. Reliability is not something that can be calculated precisely when it comes to qualitative data. However, the basic principles of reliability constitute part of all research. If data are unreliable, they will not be useful in answering your research questions. The aim is, therefore, that the data are as trustworthy as possible.

Validity

Data's validity is related to the selection and collection of data. When you are going to collect data, the questions you must ask are: 'Are the data relevant to answer the research questions?' Or have you been so selective that you ignored other data which might be of importance? For example, it is possible to make reliable measurements of the number of trips abroad the American president makes every year, but difficult to claim that this is a valid measure of the role that foreign policy issues play in American elections. It is also possible to measure the size of a person's head, but hardly possible to claim that this is a valid measurement of intelligence. Validity in research is especially important because it is difficult to know if research delivers what it promises. You cannot simply assume that the data collected in a study are valid. The scientist may have been so selective that important data are overlooked. If the scientist is working from a particular paradigm, relevant data that do not fit the paradigm may have been excluded. Or the evidence might not be relevant to the main argument and the conclusions. The aim is to collect relevant data to answer the research questions and to include all the data that are of importance.

Ethical considerations

All research conducted with human beings has ethical implications (see section 1.3). Universities and colleges have ethical standards for conducting this type of research. Many have institutionalized procedures to guarantee that informed consent is obtained by the participants in the study and that no harm will emerge as a result of their participation. It is your responsibility to know these standards and follow the university guidelines. In some instances, students must submit an application to a university committee and have their authorization before data collection can begin. This is a process that takes time. Become knowledgeable about the university standards and requirements as quickly as possible and before data collection begins.

The two main ethical issues that are related to using subjects in research are that the participants must give their fully informed consent and that they are not harmed as a result of their participation (Hart, 2008a: 277–311; Rudestam and Newton, 2007: 275–292). Informed consent is a key issue in ethical research conducted with human beings. In most cases, informed consent is required, unless you do archival or document research, secondary analyses of data, or observe people in public (e.g. on the London underground, in a busy shopping centre, at a music festival).

There are several elements in obtaining informed consent. First, provide honest information about the purpose of the study. Explain the study in a language the participants understand. They need to know what type of participation is expected of them and how long this will take. Give information about the funding of the study and the publication plans of the results. If you cannot share the purpose of the study fully because it would compromise the research, consider this issue carefully. It is your responsibility to make sure that the study does not cause problems or harm for the participants later. If the study includes children or adolescents, they require special protection. Perhaps you can share more about the purpose of the study after the questionnaire is filled out or the interview is finished. This is the time to offer to answer more questions about the study.

Second, let the participant know that participation is voluntary. In some settings, people feel pressurized to participate in order to maintain their social standing in a group or they fear that declining to participate will have negative effects on their friendships, family, studies, job situation and so on. They need to know explicitly that they are not required to participate, and that they have the right to withdraw from the study at any time without penalty. In situations where persons may experience negative effects from either participating or not participating in the study, it is important that the decision to participate, to decline to participate, and to withdraw from the study is confidential.

Third, provide information about anonymity. Anonymity means that the identity of the participant will be preserved by the researcher. For example, in a qualitative interview study, identifying information about the participant must be removed, so that neither too much information nor too little information is provided that will identify the participant. In some studies, it is not possible to provide anonymity, for example in a study of political party leaders. In this case, the participants must explicitly be informed that they will not remain anonymous in the study, and they must give their fully informed consent to the fact that identifying information about them will appear in the publications.

Finally, give information about how you plan to store the data during the study. Where and how will the data be stored? Will they be stored electronically or on paper? Who will access the data (e.g. other researchers)? What will happen to the data after the study is finished? Will they be stored or destroyed? This information is necessary for participants to make fully informed decisions to participate or not participate in your study.

Discuss with your advisor

All data have strengths and weaknesses. It is important that you understand these aspects of the data you will be collecting. Excellent books on methods will give you a lot of information on various sources of data. In addition, discuss these issues with your advisor. Is your approach the best way to find useful data? Are there other sources of data that you have not considered? What are the strengths of the data you will be collecting? What are their weaknesses? What kind of conclusions can you draw on the basis of these data? Can the findings be generalized? Your advisor will help you to understand the quality and the limitations of your data, and how to use them in the analysis.

8.4 Writing the methods chapter

Information on methods in a master's thesis gives information about what you will do to answer your research questions. Therefore, this information logically follows the presentation of the research questions. Some disciplines require that this information is written in a separate methods chapter, whereas other disciplines prefer that you incorporate this information as a section in another chapter. Find out the preferred approach within you discipline.

The aim of the methods chapter is to describe the exact steps you will take to answer the research questions. These steps must be specified in sufficient detail to allow another scientist to replicate your study. This approach is based on the ideal of the verifiability of science, meaning that scientists should be able to see if the study is conducted according to accepted methods within that particular discipline. By describing each step in detail, you will also demonstrate that you have the required methodological skills to conduct scientific research.

This does not mean, however, that the methods chapter should be written as a 'mini textbook' on methods. Some students include long sections on the differences between quantitative and qualitative research designs, which usually are quite boring. The description of the research methods must be related to the actual study that is being conducted. The idea is to describe the methodological choices you have made and the rationale for your procedures.

It is not necessarily a good idea to write this chapter before you have collected the data and completed the analysis. The reason is that you will develop methodological reflections as you go along. We recommend that you make extensive notes as you collect data and analyse them. These notes should discuss the sample, the data's reliability and validity, ethical concerns, analytical methods, assumptions on which your research rests, and the rationale of your procedures. Once you have completed the analysis, it will be relatively easy to go back to your notes and write the methods chapter. Make sure you write whole sentences and paragraphs when you take notes and not just key words. If you only use key words, it will be difficult to remember what you had in mind when you wrote them.

The structure of the methods chapter

Here we will give a brief overview of the structure of the methods chapter or methods section and mention some issues that should be addressed.

Step 1: The design of the study

A reasonable way to begin is to describe the design of the study. By 'design' we do not mean an extensive explanation of different research designs, but a short sentence or two that informs the reader of the general type of design that is used. Examples are: 'This study utilizes a representative survey design to assess the impact of integration issues in the last parliamentary election' or 'This study of unemployment is based on 25 interviews with unemployed women and men between the ages of 18 and 25 in Birmingham'. A short outline of the research design gives the reader an idea of what to expect. One example is taken from a thesis in sociology:

> This dissertation is concerned with the ways in which Muslims and Islam were conveyed in speeches by British Cabinet Ministers of the Labour Government ... For the analysis, I collected 111 speeches that were delivered by 16 different prominent Labour Ministers of the Tony Blair Cabinet between 12th September 2001 (the day after 9/11) and 27th June 2007 (the day Tony Blair resigned). (Moosavi, 2007: 6, 25)

Another example is taken from a thesis in human geography which analyses the changes in the clothing industry in Durban, South Africa. The student does not mention the data she is going to collect, but she still gives the reader an idea of what she is going to do:

> The research object of this study is the clothing industry in Durban, in the context of global competition ... The Durban area is an exciting point of departure as it is concentrated on mass-production and thus in direct competition with other low-cost areas ... By exploring the reasons behind the deteriorating competitiveness of companies and the local response, Durban might shed light to whether there are any conflicts in the relation between trade liberalisation and labour regulations in a labour-intensive industry. (Wethal, 2011: 39)

A brief description of the thesis gives the reader an understanding of what is coming.

Step 2: Discussion of challenges

The next step is to discuss the challenges you faced when attempting to answer the research questions and conduct the study. A good idea is to reiterate the research questions and then discuss the practical problems that must be resolved in order to answer them. Which research design is suitable in order to answer these questions? How do the limitations of time and money affect my choices? From where or from whom should the data be collected? What type of data should be collected? How should the data be collected? These issues might overlap with the third step below. To illustrate, we will continue to take a look at the thesis on the clothing industry in Durban. The student addresses some of the issues mentioned here:

> The chosen research method should reflect the research questions of a given project. As I wanted to get my informants' perspectives on changes and dynamics within the industry, as well as the strategies they used to confront the challenge of change, the qualitative interview was the most viable way to get the detailed information I was searching for. Through the qualitative interview, one can see the world from the informants' point of view, bring forth their experience, and reveal their perceptions. ...
>
> I stayed in Durban from the beginning of May to mid-July 2010 ... I performed 15 in-depth interviews: one with a trading house, one with a representative from the union SACTWU, one with a representative from the employer organisation NCMA, one with two representatives from the Bargaining Council, one with a consultant of textile and clothing companies, one with a manufacturer of interlining for the clothing industry, one with an official from the EThekwini municipality, five with CMT manufacturers, three with large manufacturers, as well as two conversations with my contact in the Chamber of Commerce in Durban. As shown, my informants are mostly manufacturers, but representatives from important institutions connected to the industry are also included. This gave me the opportunity to get differing and conflicting views on the status of the industry. (Wethal, 2011: 38–40)

Step 3: Procedure description

The third step is to describe the procedures. This section provides a detailed description of the exact steps you took to contact the participants in the study, obtain their consent and cooperation, and the different steps in data collection. This section will let the reader know exactly when, where and how the data were collected. If you already have provided this information in the section above, there is no need to repeat this information again. The student above said:

> I ... managed to establish a contact with the Durban Chamber of Commerce. He introduced me, by email, to a consultant for the textile and clothing companies with more than 30 years of experience from the clothing industry. These were the only

> two contacts I had when leaving … for Durban. The consultant had established an interview for me the day after our arrival in Durban and also gave me a great overall introduction to the local industry by email. The contact at the Chamber of Commerce also gave me several important contacts in the industry. These contacts assisted me with new informants. …
>
> The informant from the Chamber of Commerce could be seen as a combination of a key informant and a gatekeeper … I would not say that the informant from the Chamber of Commerce could have blocked access into the industry, but he made the entrance a lot easier, especially with the Bargaining Council, and it would have taken time to find the other informants on my own. …
>
> I also found it very useful to have a name reference when contacting a new informant.
>
> From the initial suggestions given by the contact in the Chamber of Commerce, I got new suggestions for informants. Most of my informants were obtained using this method, but I also contacted individual companies by email and phone, after a web-based search or by getting to know the company name in an earlier interview. I found this to be more challenging, as I lacked a name reference, but it still got me a few additional interviews.
>
> My field partner … assisted me in landing an interview with the trade union, and hence functioned as a gatekeeper. She had worked closely with the union for several weeks while I was focusing on manufacturers. I did not want to be related to the union before my interviews with the manufacturers were done. It turned out to be more difficult than expected to get entrance in the union. After several phone calls and visits without luck, … helped me setting up an appointment for the interview. (Wethal, 2011: 41–42)

Here, the student describes who she contacted and how easy or difficult it was to get access to informants. She also included reflections on how her informants functioned, if they were key informants or gatekeepers who opened or closed doors.

Another issue that should be discussed here is what the ethical concerns are in this study. The student above discusses in detail the issues of informed consent, confidentiality, consequences of research, and her own role as a researcher:

> I contacted my informants on the phone beforehand to inform them about the project, who I was, and what kind of information they could assist me with. At the actual interview I would emphasize that participation was voluntary. Fortunately, the informants were helpful and appeared to view the interview as a positive experience. As the interviews did not ask for any personal information, but had a theme related approach, none of the informants felt that the interview situation was intimidating or very challenging. …
>
> In the project, it was never problematic to keep my informants anonymous. Again this relates to the aim of the research – to understand the dynamics of the

industry. In presenting the views of the industry, I refer to my informants according to what kind of manufacturer they are or what kind of institution they represent. The informants were not informed about whom else I was interviewing, but most of the time they knew about some of the others because of the snowball method applied ... The struggles of the industry and the challenges they are experiencing are mostly out in the open, so that knowing of other informants would not lead to any disadvantages. ...

The informants did not see any negative consequences of being involved in the project, and they were all extremely helpful both in providing information and by assisting me in contacting other relevant informants ... One could also say that some of the informants found it relieving to talk freely about the difficulties they felt in the industry, and use their own experiences to illustrate the situation. One potential informant refused to do the interview because he was on the verge of being shut down by the Bargaining Council. Therefore, he did not want to attract negative attention to the factory or talk to anybody about his situation. In these situations it could be tempting to persuade an informant to do the interview regardless of his concerns, because it could reveal interesting information about why the company is being forced to shut down. But as it is the researcher's responsibility to protect the informants, it would not have been an option to ask him to do the interview without knowing what consequences this could have for his business. The informant was still very helpful and gave me the phone number of another informant in the same type of company. ...

It was important for me to be clear about who I was and what my project was about; a student writing a master thesis, and not somebody who could change their world. Some asked if I was a journalist, and others thought I wanted to work in the clothing industry after finalising the project. To avoid such misunderstandings I always started the interview by explaining my project, what university I came from and the field of human geography. My last question in the interview would also be if they wanted to ask me something, so that if there still were some ambiguity about the project or my status, we would clear that off before finishing ... One can never be completely sure that the informants have understood where you as a researcher are coming from, but it is important to make this information as clear as possible and an integrated part of the interview. If not, you might end up disappointing your informants at a later stage. (Wethal, 2011: 46–48)

In this description of ethical concerns, the student includes information on different ethical dilemmas she encountered during her fieldwork and how she tried to resolve them.

Step 4: Data reliability and validity
The next step is to discuss data's reliability and validity. What are the strengths and weaknesses of the data? What implications do these issues

have for the analysis? What implications do they have for the conclusions? Let us return to the student above, who reflects on some of these issues:

> This method of attaining informants can be explained as the snowball method ... A challenge with this method is that the selection of informants might come from the same network or group (Thagaard 2009). In my case, the contact from the Chamber of Commerce was particularly aware of this and gave me four contacts from distinct parts of the industry, pointing out how these four would give me different perspectives on the restructuring. You can never get completely away from possible bias with this method, as one could always question if the snowball method has excluded important informants ...
>
> As the method of qualitative research interviews is based on the premise that the data is a result of an interaction between the researcher and the informant in the interview situation, the question of replicating a project is irrelevant. Hence, the question of reliability in qualitative studies is better connected with whether or not the researcher is clear and thorough in his/her explanations about the methodological choices (Thagaard 2009). Throughout the process I have been conscious about the context in which my data has been collected, as well as having different types of informants to support or reject information from others ...
>
> Validity is linked to interpretation of the data material, and whether or not the researcher's interpretations are representative for the studied reality ... The internal validity refers to how causal relations are supported within the study. The aim of the thesis is to understand how changes in global production systems are affecting the clothing industry in Durban. By presenting a broad theoretical approach and connecting these theories with information from my informants in the analysis, I believe that I have made the causal relations within the study clear and comprehensible for the reader ...
>
> External validity is connected to transferability, meaning if and how the understanding developed in a study can have relevance for similar studies in other contexts (Thagaard 2009). One could argue that the understandings from this thesis might be transferable to other studies, as it comprises an interpretation of competitiveness and local responses in labour-intensive production. The challenges in competitiveness are likely to be present in other geographical contexts as well as other labour-intensive industries, but the response from manufacturers might differ as the possibilities for restructuring are more contextually defined. (Wethal, 2011: 42, 45–46)

Note how the student reflects on the snowball sampling she used and how she attempts to resolve the weaknesses connected to this particular data collection method. She also discusses reliability and validity.

Step 5: The analytical approach
Finally, give an outline of the analytical approach. Quantitative studies tend to include an extensive section that discusses analytical tools and strategies. This is evident in a thesis in political science on the role that foreign policy plays in American presidential elections, where the student

uses more than ten pages to describe the statistical analyses he is about to conduct (Lian, 2010: 34–46). Even if a student conducting a qualitative study may not be able to refer to specific quantitative procedures, the general framework of a qualitative analysis should be specified in the methods chapter, as both qualitative and quantitative studies involve several phases of data analysis. One example is the above-mentioned thesis in sociology which analyses the representation of Muslims and Islam in speeches by the British government:

> After acquiring the speeches, I analysed them using a discourse analysis approach, by paying close attention to the language that was deployed to construct specific meanings and then coding the most frequently-appearing aspects of the discourse into categories as necessary, to be evaluated later. Discourse analysis is based upon much of the theory developed by the philosopher Michel Foucault, most especially his development of the concept discourse. (Moosavi 2007: 25)

He continues by giving an outline of what discourse analysis is, why and how he is going to use it, and its benefits and limitations (ibid.: 25–28).

Depending upon what type of thesis you are writing, the emphasis on each of the issues discussed here will vary. Nevertheless, all of these issues are important in all science. Talk with your advisor about how much space you should use to discuss each of them.

A reminder: a common weakness in many master's theses is that students tend to write too much on how they collected the data in the methods chapter, but they include few reflections on methods in the analysis. It is important that the discussions in the methods chapter are continued in the analysis. For example, if the data have specific strengths or weaknesses, which they usually have, reflections on these aspects of the data should be included in the analysis.

8.5 Summary

1 Useful strategies to design a master's thesis:

- fill gaps in previous research
- reappraise previous research
- repeat previous research
- case studies
- write a thesis within the frames of a research programme.

2 Practical considerations in data collection:

- considering sample size with your limited time and money in mind
- checking to see if the data will be available
- collecting as reliable and relevant data as possible.

3. Ethical principles in data collection:

    - the participants must give their fully informed consent
    - they must not be harmed as a result of their participation
    - remember that many universities and colleges have ethical standards for research, and it is your responsibility to know these standards and follow them.

4. The structure of the methods chapter:

    - a description of the design of the study
    - a discussion of the challenges you face when you are going to answer the research questions and conduct the study, including ethical issues
    - a description of the procedures
    - a discussion of the data's reliability and validity
    - an outline of the analytical approach.

8.6 Action plan

You have several options when you are writing a master's thesis. Questions which you might ask are:

1. Research design:

    - Based on my research questions, what type of research design should I use? For example, I might have an interest in the changing global media industry. Looking at the research literature, what is the best approach for my study? Should I fill gaps, reappraise or repeat previous work, or conduct a case study? Or use a combination? Is there an ongoing research programme that could be relevant?
    - What are my limitations when it comes to time and money?

2. Practical and ethical considerations in data collection:

    - What is the quality of the data I am considering?
    - Have I ignored other data which might be of importance?
    - Are the data I need available?
    - How will I collect them?
    - Which ethical implications will my study have?
    - Do I need to apply for an authorization before data collection can begin?
    - How will I store the data during the data analysis?
    - What will I do with the data after my thesis is completed?

3. The methods chapter:

    - Study the methods chapter or section in a master's thesis within your discipline or go online and take a look at the master's theses that are mentioned in this chapter.
    - See how their discussions are structured.
    - Did they include all the parts mentioned in this chapter or are some missing? Learn from their strengths and mistakes.

9

The art of keeping a steady course – structuring the analysis

Analysing the data is demanding and fun at the same time. Many students feel overwhelmed when they take a look at the large amount of data they have collected and try to figure out where to start. Once they begin to write, they also discover that writing the analysis is a more lonely activity than collecting the data. The feeling of isolation can be challenging and it is important to have disciplined work habits (see section 2.4), perhaps share some of your findings on social media (section 4.1), and use the different tricks to continue writing that you know work for you (see section 3.4). At the same time, analysing data is fun because you discover new and sometimes unexpected findings and anticipate possible conclusions. During this phase, divide the tasks into manageable pieces, and take one step at a time. For example, begin by organizing the data material before you interpret and analyse them. Now is the time you will reap the benefits of working so hard to formulate specified research questions. You will discover that you can use them to create a structure for the analysis.

In this chapter, we will not discuss different analytical strategies. This information can be found in the many excellent books and other sources dedicated to quantitative and qualitative data analysis in the social sciences. Ask your teacher or advisor to help you. Our aim is to discuss various problems that most students face during this phase of the thesis. We will point out some issues we think you should be aware of to improve the analysis. However, it is important that you study relevant research literature that might be helpful when analysing your data. One idea is to take a look at the work of other scholars who use a similar analytical approach to the one you think you will use (if you have been lucky enough to have found some). Study their books or articles carefully to see how they have conducted the analysis. There is much to learn by this approach. By studying the work of acknowledged scholars, you will get ideas about how to analyse your own data.

9.1 Organizing and preparing the data for analysis

After data collection is finished, many students will have a large amount of data that seem difficult to handle. The first step is to organize and systematize the data. There are at least two reasons why you should do this before you begin the analysis. First, organizing the data will give you an overview, which will help you to see if you have the necessary data to answer your research questions. If you have collected a large amount of qualitative data, it might be difficult to get a complete overview. In some instances you will find data to questions you have not posed yet, and in other instances you discover that some data are too weak to be used. However, organizing the data will help you to see what type of information you do have. Second, getting an overview will help you to evaluate data reliability and validity. Assessing the quality of the data is important for deciding the kind of conclusions you will be able to draw (see sections 8.3 and 8.4).

There are several strategies students use to organize and systematize data, depending on the type of thesis they are doing. In many cases, to systematize data simply means to *compress* them. For example, if you have collected quantitative data, you will compress them by conducting a statistical analysis. When data are compressed, some details will disappear. This is necessary to get an overview. However, it is essential to keep enough information to answer the research questions.

When organizing and preparing qualitative data for analysis, use a system that works for you. If your data consist of text, for example transcripts from interviews, it is a good idea to classify them by using *concepts* and *categories*. This is something you can do while you are transcribing the interviews, which is usually rather boring. Make a spreadsheet on your computer and fill the top row with background variables, such as gender, age, marital status, education and profession. Continue by filling in key concepts and categories, for example views on a particular issue or development, specific practices and so on. Leave room at the end to fill in more categories and key concepts you will think of as you go along. Fill in the first column on the left with the informants' numbers or fictional names. As you transcribe the interviews, use key words to fill in information from interviews in the spreadsheet, for example that the informant is for or against a particular issue. By doing this, you are transcribing and organizing the interview data simultaneously. This will make the transcription process more interesting, and when you have transcribed all the interviews, you have a spread sheet that gives you an overview of the data. This method is useful for systematizing different types of qualitative data, such as newspaper articles, speeches, films and so on. In quantitative studies you basically use the same method by giving numerical descriptions when you code the data.

Make sure you make a different file and write down all the ideas you get for the analysis as you are organizing the data and filling in the spreadsheet. Once again, write full sentences and not just key words, so that you will be able to recapture what you had in mind when you wrote them.

Another idea for systematizing the data is to use the research questions as a frame. Let us illustrate by taking a look at a thesis we have mentioned before, namely a qualitative study of the clothing industry in Durban, South Africa (Wethal, 2011). The student posed three overall research questions in her thesis:

> What are the factors that deteriorate the competitiveness of the manufacturers in the industry and how do these affect their position in the value chain?
>
> What strategies are manufacturers in Durban using to stay competitive?
>
> How do these strategies affect employment opportunities in the Durban labour market? (ibid.: 2–4, 49, 73, 87).

The data consisted of interviews with manufacturers and representatives from important institutions connected to the industry, such as members of different governmental bodies as well as labour union and employer union representatives (ibid.: 40).

The student used the three overall research questions to systematize the data. She began by collecting the part of the material that dealt with the first research question, constraints to competitiveness. Here, she divided the data into two categories, external and internal factors that could explain the declining competitiveness. Then she used the second research question, which asked about the response of the Durban manufacturers to the new situation, to organize the material further. Once again, she divided the data by suggesting two new categories, response at the industry level and response at the company level. The data was systematized according to each of these two categories. Finally, she organized the material according to the third research question, which analysed the effects of the manufacturers' strategies on employment opportunities in Durban. Again, she used two categories to systematize the data, according to changes in the labour market and job security for unskilled workers. As demonstrated in this thesis, data are often organized and systematized several times.

When you systematize the data, remember to separate the information that appears here from your own interpretations and views. Your interpretations have a place in the analysis and the discussion later, but not during the process of organizing and preparing the data. As mentioned above, the process of systematizing data will give you ideas for analysis. Write them down for later use.

Basically, the same principle is used when systematizing quantitative data. In quantitative studies, it is important to keep methods for data analyses in mind when collecting the data, as these two processes are related. You want to make sure that the data you collect can be analysed by the statistical methods you plan to use.

9.2 Describing and interpreting the data

Of all sections, the chapters which describe, interpret and critically discuss results are the most important to write well. The committee will study them carefully because these chapters will signal your ability to make sense of data. They also reveal your ability to create consistency between theoretical discussions, research questions, methods and conclusions.

In the analysis, your job is to answer the research questions. It is a good idea to use the research questions as a frame for the analysis. We saw above how the student used the research questions to systematize the data. When she was going to write the analysis, she continued to use the research questions as a structuring frame. In the presentation, she used them as headings and under each heading she made sure she answered the questions she had posed. As an introduction to every chapter, she reiterated the research questions she was going to answer in this particular chapter (Wethal, 2011: 49, 73, 87). This helped to remind the reader of the aim of every chapter. If she had initially posed questions she was unable to find answers to in the data material, she took them out. And whenever she found interesting findings in the data on relevant questions she had not initially posed, she formulated and included them. In this way, she created coherence between the research questions and the findings she presented and discussed in this analysis.

When you describe the data and your findings, it is important that you let the *data* demonstrate that something is the way you claim it is. Many students present a claim before they have shown data which document that this is the case. It is the data, whether they consist of text, pictures, quotes from interviews, field notes or statistical data, that are your documentation. In case studies based on transcribed interview data, the convention is to quote sections of the interview verbatim. If you only narrate the evidence, by stating that 'One of the manufacturers felt that the competition was destroying his business' instead of quoting directly from the relevant transcript, you could be accused of making it up. The above narrated evidence is only a claim which needs to be supported by quoted evidence. Let us illustrate by returning to the thesis above on the clothing industry in Durban. In the analysis, this student presents several quotations from the Durban manufacturers she interviews. Below, she quotes one manufacturer who complains about the competition from China, an issue several manufacturers mention. First, she describes the context within which the manufacturers operate by referencing previous research. Then she quotes verbatim sections from the interview with one of them, before she comments at the end:

> China has both lower wages and higher productivity (Jauch & Traub-Merz 2006). While competition has heightened in lower income segments globally, imports in these segments have increased in South Africa (Velia et al. 2006). This has intensified competition for orders on the Durban market:
>
> I think it is totally unfair for local manufacturers that we're now forced to compete with the Far East and the world ... China is paying less than a third of what we're paying. (CMT manufacturer 20.05.10)
>
> The CMT manufacturer above describes a frustration among many of the producing companies in Durban. They are well aware of what is available in other countries, and see their own high input-costs as hampering competitiveness. (Wethal, 2011: 59–60)

In her comments after the quote, the student varies the description of data by paraphrasing, saying that this manufacturer 'describes a frustration among many of the producing companies in Durban' (ibid.: 60). She can do so because she has already quoted several examples from the evidence directly and shown the reader that this is a plausible narrative of the evidence. She also abbreviates the presentation by using this informant as an illustration of the views expressed by many other informants. In some cases, you might refer to data that are included in the appendices. The important issue is always that the evidence for your statements must be found in the data, and you have to demonstrate to the reader that the data support your claims.

The data will not speak for themselves, but they need to be interpreted. You have to make sense of the data by making them meaningful to the reader. This part of the thesis should therefore include both *descriptions* and *interpretations* of the data. If you conduct a quantitative study, the analysis is relatively straightforward because statistical analyses are done according to specific rules. In this type of study, it is usually a challenge to communicate clearly to the reader what the results mean and the implications they have for the study. Interpretations are therefore clearly present in quantitative studies as well.

If you conduct a qualitative study, even more space should be set aside for interpretation. In this type of study, there should be a rich *description* of each case. The reason is that this creates dynamic in the narrative. It is not enough, however, to just repeat events and statements, but the descriptions should be followed by interpretations, unless the description in itself is the interpretation. The more you describe, the more interpretation and analysis should follow.

When you interpret data, you use a perspective or frame of reference from which you make sense of the data. The perspective is found in the critical analysis of the research literature you have conducted (see Chapter 6) and drawn upon when you formulated the research questions (see Chapter 7). By now, you have discussed the literature and presented your research questions for the readers, which means that this perspective is known to them. Interpretations consist of *comparisons of similarities and differences* and *critique and discussion* of various topics. Comparing similarities and differences helps to sharpen your mind. Not all comparisons are obvious. Most of them must be discovered and developed if they are going to bring new information. It is important to ask yourself what can be useful for a comparison. Show originality by presenting new interpretations based on your understanding of the data. Critical thinking often results in new ideas. Use your own intuition and understanding of the material, which you follow up by reading.

A convention in most studies is to include a section which explains why you choose to interpret data they way you do. It is not self-evident why data should be interpreted in a particular way. You need to *justify your interpretations* by making a case for them. Specify areas that are difficult to interpret, areas of uncertainty and points of tension. For example, is more than one interpretation possible? Present the different options and provide the reasons as to why you choose the interpretations you do.

As you analyse the data, you need to include *methodological reflections and modifications*. In quantitative studies, the findings are modified based on the sample, response rate, statistical methods of analysis and so forth. In qualitative studies, you need to remind the readers and yourself that the findings only apply to the participants in the study and cannot be generalized to a larger population. A convention is also to frequently include reflections on your role and how the subjects' perceptions of you might have affected their answers.

In the discussion of findings, there should be *references back to the theoretical discussions* in the thesis, which is done by comparing your results with the results found in other studies. This will show your ability to create a direct link between theory and empirical findings, between previous research and your own work. One example which illustrates this issue is taken from the above-mentioned thesis on American presidential elections:

> The first research question raised in the introduction focused on how important foreign policy was for the vote choice of American voters. Aldrich, Sullivan and

> Borgida (1989) coined the phrase 'waltzing before a blind audience' to describe the previously prevailing view of the mismatch between the amount of time and energy presidential candidates used on foreign policy in the campaign, and the public's inability and unwillingness to care about such distant matters. This study has shown that voters certainly are not blind to the candidates' waltzing ...
>
> Although this analysis has not covered the topic of voters' level of information, it seems clear that it has further weakened the notion proposed by Almond (1960) that American voters find foreign policy questions too remote and complex to decide their vote choice. American voters have opinions on foreign policy and will use them to choose who to vote for if they find them important enough. (Lian 2010: 66)

Note how the student reiterates his first research question before he outlines the views he found in previous research, namely that voters do not care about such issues when they vote in presidential elections. He continues by concluding that his study does not support previous research but shows that voters do care about foreign policy issues.

The student above emphasizes the *differences and contrasts* between previous research and his own work. He could also have pointed out *consistency and similarities* to previous research. Usually, a study will be consistent with other research in some areas, and different from previous research in other areas. Use the outcomes of your research to nuance and develop the works of others. Does previous research suffer from errors or limitations? Or are the findings contradictive because they are based on different sources of data?

Finally, avoid taking the reader back and forth by using the same data in more than one chapter, no matter what type of structure you use in the following chapters in the analysis.

9.3 Critical analysis of the data – developing the argument

After you have described and interpreted the data, the analysis must be expanded by developing your own argument. A master's thesis usually has an overall argument which penetrates the thesis from the beginning to the end. If the argument is not clearly presented, the thesis will appear to be fragmented and unsystematic. Within any overall argument, there are also shorter and smaller attempts at stating arguments for specific issues.

Some students do not know how to develop an argument. You do not argue a specific point by describing all the findings and concluding: 'Here are all the findings, and therefore, the following must be true' (Barnes, 2005: 149). If this is all you do, you are being descriptive. However, it is you who must be critical and develop your own argument with a structure and a sequence (see section 6.4). When you are going to develop an argument, it is a good idea to begin with a context which provides limitations to the argument. From there, you present one or more propositions (see the example below). You seek to support or weaken the proposition by using the empirical findings of your study and pro-arguments, and by critically discussing relevant counter-arguments. This argumentation may lead to new propositions, which you attempt to further support or weaken. To develop an argument means to develop the logical sequence of issues that eventually leads to one or more conclusions.

In order to develop the argument you may present *two propositions*, where the purpose is to weaken one and support the other. You do this by weakening relevant counter-arguments to the proposition you want to support. However, an argument seldom consists of a discussion of two propositions. Usually, there are *a number of propositions* that could be relevant to include. To make sure that your thesis has a logical structure, the discussion should not take the reader in several different directions and end without a conclusion. Even if there are several relevant propositions, select the most important ones and argue *in favour of some* and *against the alternative and competing propositions*. We will continue to use the thesis on the clothing industry in Durban as an illustrative example. As mentioned before, one research question concerns the effects of the manufacturers' strategies on employment opportunities in Durban and the student looks at changes in the labour market and job security for unskilled workers. Under the heading 'Labour and Security,' she contextualizes the industry by first describing the South African economy from a global perspective:

> At the global arena, South Africa, with the middle-income status, finds itself competing with the highly productive developed countries and low wage countries (Theron et al. 2007). (Wethal, 2011: 92)

In order to develop her argument, the student references her critical analysis of theorists she presents earlier in her thesis. This discussion is related to the understanding of how workers and jobs are distributed unevenly in a universal market (ibid.: 20–21). Her aim is to weaken certain aspects of a theory which distinguishes between regulated and unregulated labour market segments. She first presents a central claim in the theory, which she admits can be used to describe the labour market in Durban:

> Kingdon and Knight (2007) use the insider-outsider theory of labour economists, where regulated workers can be regarded insiders, and workers in the unregulated sector and the unemployed, as outsiders. Being a highly simplistic conceptualisation of labour market segments, it can still be used to sketch insecurity in the labour market in Durban. Insiders, through Kingdon and Knight's (2007:819) conceptualisation; 'fall

> within the scope of industrial relations regulations, including recognition of trade unions and collective bargaining, the right to strike, protection against dismissal, and minimum standards concerning hours of normal and overtime work, minimum wages, and minimum leave provisions'. Outsiders naturally fall outside the formal labour regulations, and generally receive much lower income (Kingdon & Knight 2007). (Wethal, 2011: 92)

She examines the distinction between insiders and outsiders in the labour market and using it as a proposition she attempts to weaken by presenting a counter-argument:

> What this conceptualisation implies is that the insiders have secure working conditions, but it can be argued that no job is currently safe in the Durban industry. (Wethal, 2011: 92)

The student continues to support her counter-argument, namely that no job is safe in Durban, by presenting an argument of a higher order, or a pro-argument of the second order (see section 6.4):

> Hence, even with an internal segmentation of the clothing industry with regulated, semi-regulated and unregulated parts, one can argue that the whole industry is being pushed towards the outsider category. (Wethal, 2011: 92)

Her argument, that the whole industry is being pushed into the outsider category, becomes a new proposition that she attempts to support by using her own data. She quotes one of the manufacturers she has interviewed, who says:

> I don't see a future, to be honest. They'll always be there, but it'll not be in the formal sector that we are. You will see. Have you been to any Chatsworth or Clearwood factories? It'll be that sector that'll remain, but it'll be unofficial, I don't believe it'll be a council to control it, I believe they will manipulate the labour force, as far as wages and that's concerned. And it'll be very underhanded business, they'll compete with China. That's what I'm seeing...I don't see a formal sector producing, I see buying houses, I see marketing, but I can't see production (CMT manufacturer 02.06.10).
> The CMT manufacturer above explains how he perceives the future of the industry. He sees what is left of production is being moved to the unregulated sector, with low wages and high levels of insecurity for workers. (Wethal, 2011: 92–93)

Note how the student uses the quote from the manufacturer to support her proposition. Further below, she continues to argue in favour of her proposition and weaken alternative theory by claiming that it is irrelevant:

> Hence, it is impossible to place any of the segments of workers in Durban in the insider category. Because of a lack of alternatives, skills and career opportunities in

the industry, workers in Durban's clothing industry have an insecure future. Carnoy's (1980 in Beerepoot 2010) differentiation between a high-education segment, a unionized segment and a competitive segment seems irrelevant in the Durban clothing industry. The whole workforce in Durban can be described through his concept of a competitive segment; a large and poorly educated labour force competing for jobs with low and unstable working conditions, even though a large part of the workers in regulated business are unionized. (Wethal, 2011: 93)

Finally, she lets the discussion end in a conclusion by proposing an alternative theory:

Here, Friedman (2006 in Beerepoot 2010) could be more useful, as he includes a global aspect in the segmentation theory. Through his hypothesis, the threats of globalisation are so severe that only a small group of workers can secure long-term employment. (Wethal, 2011: 93)

Based on her critical analysis of theorists earlier in her thesis, Wethal argues that theories on labour segmentation in contemporary societies must include globalization as an important variable (ibid.: 21). After she has analysed the data, she brings this issue up again. In this way, she connects theory, research questions and data analysis in an overall argument that functions as a red thread in her thesis.

Another way to structure the argumentation in a thesis is to *examine several competing propositions* and point out their strengths or weaknesses by outlining the consequences of supporting or rejecting each one. The main argument is that *none* of the propositions are true, because these are the consequences. This opens up the space to present an *alternative proposition*, which is based on your findings (Barnes, 2005: 148).

Whichever way you structure the discussion, whether you use those mentioned above or you construct your own, the major issue is that you develop your conclusive argument by attempting to defend a particular statement.

9.4 Structure

Many students wonder how they should structure the analysis. A convention in theses based on quantitative data is to divide the analysis into three parts. First, present a description of data and, second, conduct the statistical analysis. The final part consists of interpretations, where the findings are critically discussed in light of the theories which are presented earlier in the thesis.

A thesis based on qualitative data does not necessarily lend itself to this structure as the three parts tend to overlap. Some advisors prefer that you go directly to the interpretations and illustrate them generously by using several quotes to illustrate. Others claim that you should let the subjects speak on their own behalf before you interpret their statements. The reasons are that this approach shows respect for the informants and enables you to distinguish between the data and your interpretations. The argument against the latter position is that your interpretations are part of the process of data selection and presentation. There is no perfect way to structure the analysis. Whichever way you choose, you must describe what you have done and why you choose to structure it the way you do. Perhaps the readers will not agree with you, but they will be satisfied if you make a good case.

9.5 Coherence

Consistency in the thesis is created by having each part stand in a logical relationship to the other parts, so that together they create a totality. Consistency is created within each chapter by including introductions and summaries. In the beginning of a chapter, let the reader know what is coming and how it is connected to the rest of the thesis. At the end of the chapter, summarize briefly what you have discussed. Cross-references in the text can also be used to create coherence between the different parts. It is much better that you reference back to something you wrote before than frequently present promises of what is to come later.

Consistency is further created within each chapter by grouping different ideas, comparisons and discussions. Nothing should stand in isolation. Look at your text and ask 'Where is the connection with the rest?'. As you come to the end of the analysis, it is extremely important to see how each part is consistent with the central ideas. Make sure you have not moved so far from the beginning that the early texts seem irrelevant. From the beginning to the end, the thesis should be coherent to the degree that it makes sense as a whole.

9.6 Inclusive and bias-free writing

We would like to end this chapter with some ethical considerations in writing (see Rudestam and Newton, 2007: 282–292). Throughout the entire thesis, it is important to avoid phrases and words which discriminate or oppress different groups. Every questionnaire, every interview guide and text should be examined carefully to ensure that there are no direct or indirect references which suggest that it is 'normal' or 'correct' to belong to a specific ethnic group, gender, age, religion, or have specific sexual preferences.

As an author, you have an obligation to keep up to date on how different phrases and words might be perceived by various groups. Changes are constantly made in this area, and what was acceptable language yesterday might not be so today. We will mention a few rules you can use to avoid writing in such a way that you condone and reproduce prejudices:

- Use gender-neutral instead of gender-specific words. Avoid using 'he', instead write 'she or he'. The text can become difficult and awkward if you frequently use the latter, so it might be better to change it to plural and say 'they'. Another solution is to change to 'one' or 'you'.
- Do not simply assume that one profession includes only one gender. Examples would be to write 'the researcher ... he' or 'the pre-school teacher ... she'.
- Avoid gender stereotypes, for example 'a good and beautiful female student' and 'an intelligent and cool male professor'.
- Do not identify people according to ethnicity unless it is relevant. If it is relevant, use the phrases and words which are accepted by the groups you reference.
- Avoid language which degrades others or reinforces stereotypes. For example, statements which refer to a group as 'culturally deprived' or that someone has 'a religion which is inconsistent with modern society' are degrading.
- Avoid hegemonic language. There are several words and phrases which reflect a form of dominance. Words like 'we' and 'the others' in descriptions of ethnic, religious or sexual groups have hegemonic functions. Even in situations where words like 'the others' are used ironically, they might reflect a form of dominance.
- Avoid paternalistic language. For example, the phrase 'my informants' might suggest that you are somehow in a relationship of ownership to the subjects in your study. Instead, use the phrase 'the informants in this study', 'the subjects in this study' or 'the participants in my study.'
- Do not present undocumented assumptions about different age groups, for example, 'the elderly are surprisingly able to work longer than they used to'.

9.7 Summary

1 The data must be organized and systemized several times before you interpret them. Data can be systematized:

- by being compressed
- according to concepts and categories
- by the research questions.

2 The research questions should be used to frame the analysis.
3 In the description and interpretation of data:

- let the data demonstrate that something is the way you claim it is
- develop originality in the interpretations
- include methodological reflections

- include references to theory
- emphasize differences and contrasts, as well as consistency and similarities.

4 A critical discussion of the data should include:

- a penetrating argument from beginning to end
- a discussion of the most important propositions with pro- and counter-arguments.

5 Use the following list to see if you have avoided common mistakes in your argumentation. According to Barnes (2005: 150), a bad argument may include statements which:

- contradict themselves
- have no relationship with previous statements
- do not have any logical sequence
- are based on assumptions that were never questioned
- appeal to authorities that are known to be limited or suspect (dictionaries, historical traditions long discredited, research now challenged, famous people, writers of fiction)
- present opinion as argument unsupported by evidence
- contain nothing that leads to a logical conclusion
- take no account of exceptions or counter-claims
- try to claim absolute instead of qualified truths.

6 Consistency in a thesis should be created within each chapter and between all the chapters.
7 The language should be inclusive and bias-free.

9.8 Action plan

1 Begin by writing one chapter of the analysis and work thoroughly with this chapter. It is easier to write a text of 10–15 pages rather than 100 pages!
2 First, describe and interpret the data:

- reiterate the research questions you are going to answer in this chapter
- compare similarities, differences and contrasts
- develop new and original interpretations
- justify your interpretations
- place your findings in the context of your critical analysis of theory.

3 Critically analyse your data and develop an overall argumentation:

- select one or two important propositions
- argue in favour of some and against others
- formulate conclusions that stand in a logical relationship to the argumentation.

4 Check to see that there is consistency within this chapter.
5 Make sure you use bias-free language.
6 After you have written one chapter of analysis, confer with your advisor. If necessary, revise and resubmit. Once this chapter has an acceptable form, use it as a standard for the remaining chapters in the analysis.

10

Beginning and end – introduction and conclusion

The first and the last chapters of the thesis are important. The introduction gives the reader a taste of what is to come. Here you have a chance to spark interest and grab the attention of the reader. You should give just the right amount of information to entice the reader into your thoughts about the thesis topic. The conclusion is your final chance to influence the reader in the direction you want. These two parts of the thesis are connected. In the final chapter you return to the questions you posed in the introduction and give the 'essence' of the conclusions.

10.1 The introduction

Although the introduction is placed at the beginning of the thesis, it is possible to write it later. Some suggest that you leave writing the introduction until the end, and then write it simultaneously with the summary and conclusions, because it is impossible to write a final introduction chapter prior to completing the thesis. Others think that writing a draft of your introduction and revising it as you go along is a better idea, because this helps to organize your thoughts. Whichever way you choose, you will most likely rewrite and edit the introduction several times.

The introduction offers a broad context for your study. You tell the reader exactly what you are going to write about. This is your opportunity to set the intellectual level of your thesis. You do yourself no favours by beginning in a way that creates a poor first impression, so be prepared to put effort into writing a good introduction. It should leave the reader in no doubt about the purpose of your thesis and how it will unfold.

If you do not know how to structure the introduction, study carefully one of the master's theses which are referenced in this book and available online. One example is a thesis in education which studies pupil resistance to authority (Fortune, 2010). Here, we will give a brief overview of the type of information commonly found in introductions. First, present the *topic of the thesis*. Readers get bored very quickly if you present long overviews of theories or research traditions without letting them know the purpose of this information. Create a context for the reader by explaining what the thesis is about. Second, narrow the focus by presenting *the research questions*. The wording of the research questions should be sufficiently explicit to orient any reader. Make sure you include the overall questions as well as the specified questions. Third, give information about the *purpose of the thesis*. You want to say something about why you are writing about this topic. Explain the rationale or the justification for why these questions deserve the attention of the reader.

The next step is to present *the scientific and theoretical approach*. What do we already know about the topic? By referencing established research, the reader is left with the impression that you have taken notice and considered other sources of authority from the beginning. An early sideways glance at existing research shows evidence of wide reading and qualitative work. Furthermore, give a brief *presentation of the literature* that will be discussed, followed by an outline of *the methods used in the study* or the procedures used to explore the research questions. Describe briefly the study by providing information about data, sample and data collection. Then, discuss the *methods of analysis* that have been applied. Conclude the introduction by presenting a *reading map* where you outline the structure of the thesis and the content of the chapters that follow.

10.2 The conclusions chapter

The final chapter is the place you tell the reader what you have achieved in your study. This chapter is based solely on the contents of the previous chapters, so do not introduce anything new here. The conclusions should follow logically from the previous analysis and discussion and appear to be evident to the reader. Just as it might be useful to see how other students have structured an introduction, it may be helpful to study how they have written the conclusions. Again, study some of the theses used as examples in this book, or take a look at the thesis in education mentioned above, which has a section at the end where many of the issues mentioned here are included (Fortune, 2010: 338–348).

The conclusions chapter usually consists of several sections. First, provide a *summary*. Reiterate the overall and the specified research questions and the data you analysed to answer these questions. What were the main findings? Give an outline of the main results from your study. Emphasize the most important issues and explain why this is important. Include statements that evaluate if and how the research objectives have been fulfilled. If changes were made to the original research design, explain why. Often some results come as a surprise. If so, describe and discuss the results you expected to find and the ones that were unexpected.

Further, present *conclusions* about your findings. The conclusions will often be part of the summary. Answer the research questions in a way that is sufficiently clear to inform any reader. If the thesis is structured in a way that tests one or more alternative hypotheses, evaluate the strengths of the hypotheses. State explicitly if the hypotheses were weakened, strengthened or should be modified. Finally, present the explanations of your conclusions and discuss other possible explanations.

State the relationship of your study to the *research literature*. Describe how the results contribute to understanding the phenomenon and the implications of the findings for existing research. This means that you may critique the interpretations, assumptions or concepts used in previous research, and use your study to develop them further. This is how your research may have *theoretical implications*.

Comment on the limitations of your research. Discuss the strengths and weaknesses of the study. This information may contribute to developing future research. Include suggestions for improvements, in case you were to follow up with another study later.

Finally, conclude by discussing *implications for future research*. Good research tends to lead to puzzles and new research questions. This may mean that you identify topics that need further study, concepts that must be elaborated and refined, or gaps in research that should be filled. On the basis of the work you have done, what type of research would you recommend?

10.3 Summary

1. The introduction should include:
    - a presentation of the topic of the thesis
    - the research questions
    - the purpose of the thesis
    - the scientific and theoretical approach
    - a brief presentation of the research literature
    - the methods

- the analytical approach
- a reading map of the thesis.

2 The concluding chapter should include:

- a summary of the research questions, methods and findings
- the explanations of the conclusions
- the implications for existing research
- the limitations of your research
- implications for further research.

10.4 Action plan

1 Write a first draft of your introduction. Revise and edit it by asking yourself questions like these:

- Is the topic of the thesis presented early in the introduction?
- Are the research questions posed explicitly?
- Is the rationale for the research questions explained?
- Are the scientific and theoretical frames of approach presented?
- Is there a description of the research literature you are going to discuss?
- Is the choice of data and methods described?
- What about the analytical approach?
- Finally, is a reading map included?

2 Do the same as above and use the following questions as a checklist:

- Are the overall and the specified research questions reiterated?
- Is there a summary of main findings from your study?
- Are there explicit conclusions that answer the research questions?
- What are the scientific and theoretical implications of your study?
- What are the limitations?
- Which recommendations do you propose for future research?

11
Chaos and order – editing and referencing

Even if we discuss editing towards the end of this book, editing is an activity that should take place throughout the entire writing process. From the beginning, get used to the idea that what you write will be edited and reworked many times. Drafting, writing, rewriting, proofing and editing are part of the writing process and soon become routine (see section 3.5). At the end of the process, there is a need to go over the entire thesis. After all the chapters have been written, some students start to run out of time and are tempted to skip editing. A poor composition or format will, however, be reflected in your grade. The first complete draft of your thesis is most likely in need of editing. Here is your real opportunity to give your thesis final shape and emphasis.

Editing can sometimes be painful. Giving your writing emphasis means to push some parts of the text into the background and pull other parts forward. Perhaps you realize that you have written too much and you must leave out the part of the text you laboured with and truly like. Reducing and taking out text is part of the writing process. This does not mean, however, that you delete it: it is a good idea to make new files and organize the text according to relevant key words so that you can find it later. You may use this material for something else, for example in a lecture or an article.

11.1 A classic thesis structure

We have previously mentioned that a thesis should have unity and coherence (see section 9.4). The different parts of the thesis should be connected.

As we outline a typical thesis structure, you will see that a thesis has a beginning, a middle section and an end. Each section and all the parts should be interrelated. A thesis usually has a plot or a narrative structure (Hart, 2008a: 101–102), in the sense that it tells the story of a problem you found, which some scholars believed was important and which you thought was interesting, so this is what you did and what you found, and this is why it is important.

The different parts of a thesis are often placed in a given order. The final manuscript also contains additional parts, which are meant to provide important information and help the reader navigate the text. Here, we will give an outline for a classic structure (Barnes, 2005: 135–136). Your version might not follow this structure, but the format is common. The suggested percentages of text are a very rough guide. Talk to your advisor about the final draft and find out how it should look.

Front page	Give a short title with a more specified subtitle, author, year and place of study.
Summary	A brief summary of the whole thesis.
Contents	Headings and sub-headings with page numbers.
Acknowledgements	Thanks to advisor and other relevant persons and institutions.
Introduction	A presentation of the thesis topic, why this study is important, its practical and theoretical significance, an outline of the research questions (overall and specified), data, methods of analysis and an outline of content. (10 per cent)
Research literature	The descriptive overview of the relevant research literature in the field is followed by critical analysis and discussions of key issues. Sometimes this is a separate chapter. Others slice the description and analysis of the literature in the text so that the literature review permeates the writing. (20 per cent)
Research questions and methods	Presentation, rationale and specification of the research questions. Presentation of method(s) and the reasons for using these methods, based on the research questions. (20 per cent)
Analysis	Presentation and interpretations of the data. Results, findings, including tables, graphics and statistics. (25 per cent)
Discussion and critique	Critical analysis, discussion and critique of the results and findings. (15 per cent)
Summary/conclusion	Summary of the findings, limitations of the research: strength and weaknesses, and implications for future research. (10 per cent)

| References | Alphabetical list of references that occur in the text. |
| Appendices | Where appropriate: samples of interview guide, questionnaires and so on. |

The size of a master's thesis varies according to different disciplines. Find out the requirements at your university. Exceeding the word count is often a problem. Use the classic thesis structure above and look at your thesis. Where is the imbalance? Some students use too much space on the description of theory and not enough on the discussion. Others write a lengthy description and interpretation of data, but include hardly any critical analysis. Trimming the word count can usually be done in the descriptive parts of the thesis, such as the description of theory and the description of data.

11.2 Quotations

Finding a really good quotation is not difficult, but using it well in the text is not that easy. Often students want to quote an author directly because they think that the issue is well stated. Within the academic genre, it is more common to paraphrase, or put the quoted material into your own words, and reference the source than to use direct quotations. The purpose of quotations is to support a point and illustrate the text. As a general rule, avoid long quotations, as they are not meant to carry the text. If you follow these guidelines, you will avoid delivering a text with long quotations and little text in between. Also, when paraphrasing the text, do not copy any of the text, as this is plagiarism and unethical behaviour – to be avoided at all cost.

Exceptions to this rule are found in empirical studies and master's theses based on qualitative data collected by the author. A common strategy in these studies is to use long quotations to give the subjects space to formulate the issue at hand in their own words, and to place their statements in a larger context. These quotations refer to the data. Sometimes it is necessary with long quotations to demonstrate to the reader that the interpretations are reasonable. A similar example is this book, where we have used long quotations from completed master's theses to illustrate how students actually go about writing. However, be aware that in some instances you will need permission to quote.

Sometimes students want to quote sections of a text. If you exclude parts of the text in a quotation, use three dots followed by a full stop if it is at the end of a sentence .... Quotations which are less than five lines should be integrated in the text, with quotation marks in the beginning and the end. For example: 'Slavery had a traumatic impact on both genders and on all aspects of life for the Africans brought over to America' (Patterson, 1998: 26). Longer quotations should be separated from the main body of the text and block indented (not just the first line) without quotations marks. The reference is placed within parenthesis at the end of the quotation and should include author name(s), date of publication and page.

Remember to write the quotation in the language you found it written, unless it is a language few people understand. If you translate the quotation, indicate that you have done so. For example: (Bourdieu, 1986: 69, transl. by the author).

11.3 Notes

Notes are used to give additional information that for some reason does not fit with the text. They are not used for references to literature. There are really no definite rules when it comes to notes. Whereas some authors like to use notes, other authors do not use notes at all. The type of additional information often found in notes is a continuation of a debate that is too detailed to be included in the text. Notes are also used to add relevant information that will burden the text, such as factual information. A general rule is that if the information is so important that it must be included, it should be included in the text. In other words, try to limit the use of notes.

Notes are usually placed at the end of the text or at the bottom of the page (like a footnote). In the first case, the notes are placed at the end of the text, but before the references. This is relatively common in articles. In the second case, notes are placed at the bottom of the page to make location easier, which is common in larger studies, like a master's thesis.

11.4 References

The purpose of referencing is related to the ideal of research as a collective project. Research is largely built upon the work of other scholars, and referencing is used to acknowledge their work. An important principle is to respect the scholars who came before you. Copying the ideas of others and using them as if they were your own is plagiarism and is a breach of scholarly ethics. It should be evident in the text if the ideas and information are taken from other scholars or if they are your own. Referencing previous research is also used to justify your writing and give it substance. References in the text mean that there are evidence and support for your statements in other books or articles that can be found if the reader wishes to do so. Finally, referencing is used to demonstrate to the reader that you know the research literature in the field. A text with many references is often a sign of a well-read author.

This does not mean that you should burden the text with irrelevant references. There are two main rules regarding referencing literature. First, only include important, published references. References to unpublished data are usually placed in the notes. References to newspaper articles are often placed in a bracket with the name of the newspaper and full date at the end of a sentence (see section 11.5). Second, check that the references are correct on the basis of the original publication. If you copy the references of others, you risk copying their mistakes; this is easily detected by someone who is well read in the field.

There are several different styles for listing references at the end of your thesis. The departments at your university have different traditions, and publishers and journals have their ways of doing it. The various reference styles vary according to the amount of information included and the order in which it is presented. For example, whereas most reference styles include the title of the article, some do not. Also, some systems list the date of publication after the name of the author, whereas others list it at the very end. Use the reference style recommended at your university, and take care to follow it systematically.

Writing references is tedious work and takes a lot of time. It is therefore important to take detailed bibliographic notes whenever you read something that might be of use later (see section 5.9 on keeping a search log). These notes should be as complete as possible. Write down the author's full name, complete title of the publication, pagination of articles, date of publication, publisher and place of publication. By doing so, you will have all the necessary information to write the references. In your thesis, you will be writing the references according to the style recommended by your university. If you are going to publish an article based on your thesis later, you might have to change the references to a different style. It is easier to edit a complete list of references than to find new information because some information is missing.

Since writing references is so time consuming, we advise you to write it as you go along and not wait until the end. Several students have learned this the hard way and waited until the end, only to discover that the information they had about a given source was incomplete and almost impossible to find. Our advice is to end your day by writing down all new references. Either write references in a separate file or use the bibliographic programmes or systems that are available on the Internet (see section 5.9).

After you have written the thesis, go back and edit the references. Even if you have carefully written down references as you go along, you may have included mistakes or find that some information is missing. Use the library OPAC (see section 5.5) to get the information you need.

11.5 Referencing in the text

The most common way of referencing is to use the 'author–date' style, which means placing the author's last name, followed by the date of publication and page number, within parentheses. In the *references* section at the end of the thesis, your references should be listed alphabetically by name of author. The advantage of this system is that the reader will find the name and the date of the reference without difficulty. The disadvantages are that several references in the text will make the reading more difficult, and that the reader must look at the end of thesis to find the full reference. Whether you use a colon or a comma is a matter of style (see section 11.7), but be consistent and never mix different styles.

References in the text are usually made in two ways:

1 If the author's name is in the text, it is followed by the date of publication, and in some instances the page number, within parentheses. For example: 'Patterson (1998: 25) claims that slavery destroyed the Afro-American family structure in such a way that it still affects Afro-American women and men.'
2 If the authors name is not in the text, but you give a summary of the author's view, end the sentence with the author's last name, date of publication and page number within parentheses. For example: 'Slavery destroyed the possibility to be a husband and a father. Since the slave was reduced in law and civic life to a nonperson, a man could not have authority or power over his children or their mother (Patterson, 1998: 27).'

The 'author–date' style of referencing differs depending upon the number of authors, the number of publications and so forth. Here are some examples:

- One author, one publication: (Patterson, 1998)
- One author, several publications: (Patterson, 1997, 1998)
- One author, several publications published the same year (distinguish each reference by using letters a, b etc.): (Bourdieu, 1971a, 1971b)
- Several authors: (Frazier, 1963; Kivisto, 1993; Wood 2006)
- Two authors, the same publication: (Ebaugh and Chafetz, 2000)
- Two or more authors, the same publication: (Alba et al., 2008)
- One author, quoted by another author: (Peirce, quoted by Eco, 1979a: 69)
- Recommending further reading: (see Calhoun, 2007)

Whatever style you use, be consistent and pay attention to the use of commas, colons, semi-colons and full-stops.

References are listed in full at the end of your thesis, and they are always in alphabetical order. The references must have been mentioned in the text. In order to check the consistency between references in the text and the list at the end, print first the list of references, then go back to the beginning of the document and search for the first parenthesis sign – as in: (– and this will take you to the first text reference. Check this on your list of references to make sure the name and date are correct, or add full details for those that are missing. Repeat the process to the end of the document. Finally, delete all the references in the list that are not mentioned in the text.

11.6 Referencing electronic sources

There are several different electronic sources, such as websites, electronic databases, software or electronic journal articles, and different rules apply for referencing these types of sources. The *Harvard Style of Referencing* is used by many (see University Library, 2011). However, there are several other styles as well, for example the *Chicago Manual Style* (www.chicagomanualofstyle.org/home.html). Again, use the style manual recommended by your university. Below we offer you some information about the elements that usually should be included when referencing electronic sources.

Websites

To determine the author or source of a website can be difficult. If the website is a company or a public institution, reference the corporate authorship. Information about date of publication also varies on different websites. Give the last updated date, if available. If there is no date, use the date you accessed the information. In some cases, the reference is to a document on a general website. Here, give the title of the web page or web document, which you find at the top of the screen. When you are going to reference an electronic source, give information about the type of medium this is, for example 'online', if you have downloaded it from the Internet, or 'e-book' or 'PDF'.

Information about publisher and place of publication is irrelevant when it comes to websites. Instead, give the reader information about where to find the electronic information, the website address or URL (uniform resource locator). It is not enough to reference a website, as many will have problems finding the link. Instead, include information about where the website is available. Do so by copying the URL from the net rather than writing it yourself. It is easy to make small mistakes, which prevents the reader from finding it.

The information on the Internet constantly changes. A document found today can be moved to another address tomorrow or disappear completely. For this reason, include the date (day/month/year) for when the document was accessed.

In contrast to printed media, electronic sources do not have clearly defined pages. Therefore, do not give information about pagination, even if it appears when you print the document. Only use page numbers when referencing an

Acrobat document. Acrobat documents (or PDFs) are photographic copies of original printed sources and do have page numbers. You will recognize a PDF, since it is only readable by using the Adobe Acrobat Reader program, which can be downloaded for free on the Internet. Based on what we have said so far, the elements for referencing a website are, for example:

American Psychological Association 2010. *Ethical Principles of Psychologists and Code of Conduct* [online]. Available at: www.apa.org/ethics/code/index.aspx [Accessed 26 February 2012].

Publications found on the Internet

Many publications are available online, such as e-books, academic journal articles, master's theses, PhD dissertations and public documents. Unless the document is a journal article, give information about place of publication and publisher. If is it is a journal article, include the name of the journal, volume and issue number. Many publications on the Internet are available in PDF format, which means that information about pagination should be included. The elements for an article in an electronic journal are, for example:

Gaye, A. and Jha, S., 2011. Measuring Women's Empowerment through Migration. *Diversities* 13(1), s. 49–66 [pdf]. Available at: http://unesdoc.unesco.org/images/0019/001914/191499e.pdf#191551 [Accessed 26 February 2012].

11.7 List of references

The full list of references is at the end of your thesis and the references are always in alphabetical order. It is expected that you will have a complete and correct list of references. It is a good idea to copy a reference list and study it in great detail for every reference until you have learned the manual style.

Be aware that different sources are listed in different ways. For example, there are different set-ups for books, articles in journals, articles in books, publications from an organization or an institution, unpublished theses and so on. A general rule is that a reference should be listed as it appears in its original version. For example, some journals use capital letters in the main words of the title of the article, some do not.

11.8 Summary

1 When near completion, the entire thesis must be read from beginning to end.
2 The size requirement for a thesis varies from discipline to discipline.

3. There is a classic thesis structure that can be used to trim the word count.
4. Quotations should be short, unless the quotation refers to the data.
5. The use of notes should be limited.
6. Every university has a recommended reference style.
7. The full list of references is at the end of the thesis and in alphabetical order.

11.9 Action plan

1. Editing the thesis. Take a look at the first full draft of your thesis:
   - Which parts are too large and must be abbreviated?
   - Which parts are too small and should be expanded?
   - Which parts are still missing?

2. Look at all the quotations and notes:
   - Are all the quotations meaningful and integrated into the text?
   - Should some notes be longer, shorter or deleted?

3. Find out the approved reference manual at your university:
   - Practise every day by writing correct references in the text and in the reference list.

12
When is it finished? Checklist summary

Many students are tired towards the end. You have lived with the thesis for a long time. It might be difficult to get the necessary distance to finish the work. There are always some parts of the text that should be improved and rewritten. Perhaps a chapter did not turn out the way you had in mind or the literature review is less extensive than you thought. Perhaps the thesis is not the 'masterpiece' you envisioned. However, at one point it is important to finish it, submit it, and move on with life. The problem might be that it is difficult to know when it is finished. Here we will take a look at what to do towards the end of the writing process.

12.1 Reading the thesis with a critical eye

During the work with the thesis – and especially when the analysis is coming to an end – it is important that you set a deadline for when you are going to submit the thesis (see section 1.4). Once you have a date, plan the weeks before the deadline carefully. Make sure you set aside time for editing. Towards the end, you will find that you will be able to get a lot of work done in just one week.

Since you are the one who has the final responsibility for the thesis, you must read it carefully from the beginning to the end. Below, we have included a checklist you may use for each section of the thesis.

Look for the following throughout the thesis
- Do you go from the general to the specific?
- How do you structure paragraphs and sentences?

➡

- Do the topic sentences state the controlling ideas in the paragraphs?
- Are the sentences precise?
- Is the text consistent and coherent?
- Do some parts stand alone and in isolation from the rest?

The introduction

- Does the introduction offer a broad context for your study?
- Do you clearly present the topic of the thesis?
- Do you present the research questions and the purpose of the thesis?
- Remember to briefly describe the research literature, data and methods of analysis.
- Include a brief reading map to the entire thesis.

The review of the research literature

- Do you include literature that appears to be necessary to understand the topic of your thesis?
- Do you give more space to the literature than is important to your own argumentation?
- Do you critically evaluate and analyse the literature?
- Do you discuss the important issues in the field?
- Are these issues relevant to your research questions?
- How is your argumentation structured?
- Do you formulate propositions that are debated by using pro- and counter-arguments?
- Is the argumentation coherent or does it go in many different directions?
- Are your arguments valid, significant and correct?

The research questions

- Have you formulated the overall research questions?
- What are the rationales for the questions?
- Do you have theoretical or practical rationales, or both?
- Are the research questions specified in such a way that they indicate the observations that must be made to answer the questions?
- Is there coherence between the research questions and the critical analysis of the research literature?

The research method

- Is there consistency between the research questions and the research methods?
- Have you explained why the research methods are adequate?
- Have you included a discussion of the methodological strengths and weaknesses?
- Have you remembered to comment on the sample and the validity and the reliability of the data?
- Does your thesis raise ethical issues that must be discussed?

The analysis

- It is important to check that you have answered all the research questions. Make sure that there is consistency between the research questions and the analysis.
- Check that all statements of fact are supported by the data.
- Remember not to use identical data in more than one chapter.
- How do you explain and justify your interpretations?
- Have you remembered to critically analyse and discuss your findings?
- Do you refer to the theoretical debates in your discussion of the findings?
- Is your overall argumentation evident for the reader?
- Check that no part stands alone or in isolation from the rest. Are the different parts connected and is there is a 'red thread' going through the entire analysis?
- Make sure that the analysis is consistent with the purpose and the aims of the study.

Summary and conclusions

- Check that you have repeated the research questions and described the research methods you used to answer the questions.
- Make sure that all the findings are summarized.
- Have you answered all the research questions you posed in the introduction and later in the thesis?
- Remember to present the explanations of the findings and the theoretical implications of your study.
- Have you included comments on the strengths and weaknesses of your study?
- Check that there is consistency between the introduction and the conclusions chapter.
- Include a few suggestions for further study.

References in the text

- Are the references correct and complete?
- Are the references in the text consistent with the list of references?

List of references

- Which manual style have you used? Have you followed it systematically?
- Is the reference list correct? Read it carefully.

Editing the different parts of the thesis

- Does the composition of the thesis give a balanced impression? Or does the thesis seem imbalanced where some parts are too large or too small?

Grammar and spelling

There is no reason to let your thesis suffer from poor spelling. Use the spell-check on your computer. In addition, read the entire thesis carefully. For example, the spell-check will approve both 'you' and 'me', but the meaning is different. You have rewritten the thesis, or parts of it, several times. It is easy to overlook parts of previous versions that should have been deleted, or perhaps you deleted that which should be included. Sometimes, you have read the text so many times that you are blinded and overlook mistakes. It is a good idea to get a fellow student or another competent reader to read your final draft before you send it to your advisor.

12.2 Comments and approval from your advisors

About one or two months before you submit your thesis, send a first complete draft to your advisor, or advisors if you have more than one. A complete draft consists of all parts of the thesis, from front page and contents to references and appendices. So far, your advisors have only read individual chapters or parts of the thesis. It is not easy to remember in detail what the theoretical part, written a semester ago, looks like and know if it fits with the rest of the thesis. By reading a complete draft, your advisors will be able to look at the complete thesis and its composition. Should some parts be expanded or should some parts be trimmed?

Talk with your advisors about the date for the first complete draft, so that they will have enough time to read it carefully. Although we recommend one to two months before the final deadline, this is something you and your advisors decide. If the complete draft is fairly well composed, perhaps a month is enough for your advisors to read it carefully, and for you to make the necessary corrections.

Listen carefully to the comments of your advisors. At this point, many students are so tired of the whole thesis that they are tempted not to do the final editing. Do not give in to these temptations, as it would be silly to spoil your chances of a good grade after all the effort you have put into your thesis so far. It is important to remember that you, as a student, are the one who has the final responsibility for the thesis. If you get a poor grade, it is your responsibility, and you cannot blame your advisors. Therefore it is important that you set aside time to make the final corrections. Some theses improve incredibly by relatively simple editing towards the end.

12.3 Work in progress

As we are at the end of this book, we hope that you as a reader will ask many questions about our approach. This is the attitude we want to encourage. If you, by reading a section or a chapter in this book, are better prepared and have more success with your master's thesis than you would otherwise, we will have added something of value to you. We expect you to disagree with us at times. However, if we have inspired a discussion of writing in general and writing a master's thesis more specifically, we have done our job. We have not tried to teach you the *only* way to writing, but to inspire thought and encourage search for the most effective way to do this, premised on your skills.

This book has been edited, read and critiqued by several colleagues. We have rewritten the text, deleted some, moved other parts, and added new text. In this way, our book is also a text that can be improved. Our hope is, however, that this edition will help you as a student to develop your skills, so that you are more effective and less stressed about the writing process.

References

Barnes, R., 2005. Successful Study for Degrees, 3rd edn. London and New York: Routledge.

Barrass, R., 2002. Scientists Must Write: A Guide to Better Writing for Scientists, Engineers and Students. London and New York: Routledge.

Bitsch, A., 2010. The Geography of Rape: Spaces of Shame and Risk. MA thesis, University of Oslo. Available from: www.duo.uio.no/publ/iss/2010/105279/bitsch.pdf (accessed 23 April 2011).

Bolton, R., 1986. People Skills: How to Assert Yourself, Listen to Others, and Resolve Conflicts. New York: Simon & Schuster.

Brady, J., 2010. Electric Car Cultures: An Ethnography of the Everyday Use of Electric Vehicles in the UK. MA thesis, Durham University. Available from: http://etheses.dur.ac.uk/690/ (accessed 14 July 2012).

Brennan, J.H., 1990. How to Get Where You Want to Go. Wellingborough: Thorsons.

Creswell, J.W., 2008. Research Design: Qualitative, Quantitative, and Mixed-Methods Approaches. London: Sage.

Crotty, M., 1998. The Foundations of Social Research: Meaning and Perspective in the Research Process. London: Sage.

Elbow, P., 1981. Writing with Power: Techniques for Mastering the Writing Process. New York and Oxford: Oxford University Press.

Fortune, S., 2010. A Critical Ethnography of Pupil Resistance to Authority: How Pupil and Teacher Identities Create Spaces of Resistance in the Contemporary School. MA thesis, Durham University. Available from: http://etheses.dur.ac.uk/548/ (accessed 14 July 2012).

Gallo, J.D. and Rink, H.W., 1991. Shaping College Writing: Paragraph and Essay, 5th edn. New York: Harcourt, Brace.

Gustavsen, A., 2010. Not Welcome Here: Local Liverpool Fan's Experience of Recent Commercial Changes in English Football. MA thesis, University of Oslo. Available from: www.duo.uio.no/sok/work.html?WORKID=101039 (accessed 17 April 2011).

Gustavsen, E., 2011. Siblings in Arms? Gender Perspectives in the Norwegian and US Armed Forces. MA thesis, University of Oslo. Available from: www.duo.uio.no/publ/iss/2011/119036/Gustavsen.pdf (accessed 27 July 2011).

Hansen, J., 2007. I Carried My Sorrow Songs: The Expression of Dissent and Social Protest in the Blues and Hip Hop. MA thesis, University of Oslo. Available from: www.duo.uio.no/publ/ILOS/2007/57977/masterthesis.pdf (accessed 17 April 2011).

Hart, C., 2008a. Doing your Masters Dissertation. London: Sage.

Hart, C., 2008b. Doing a Literature Search. London: Sage.

Haug, B., 2009. Educational Decentralization and Student Achievement: A Comparative Study Utilizing Data from PISA to Investigate a Potential Relationship between School

Autonomy and Student Performance in Australia, Canada, Finland, Norway and Sweden. MA thesis, University of Oslo. Available from: www.duo.uio.no/sok/work.html?WORKID=91354 (accessed 23 April 2011).

Hermansen, A.S., 2009. Unmaking the Vertical Mosaic? Occupational Class Attainment among Second-Generation Immigrants to Norway. MA thesis, University of Oslo. Available from: www.duo.uio.no/sok/work.html?WORKID=96934 (accessed 17 April 2011).

Herron, R.C., 2010. Superficially Similar but Fundamentally Different: A Comparative Analysis of US and UK Affirmative Action. MA thesis, Durham University. Available from: http://etheses.dur.ac.uk/662/ (accessed 1 July 2012).

Hestad, K.A., 2008. Docile Bodies, Reflective Selves. A Foucauldian-Somatic Perspective on Symbolic Interactionism. MA thesis, University of Oslo. Available from: www.duo.uio.no/publ/iss/2008/75751/Hestad.pdf (accessed 23 April 2011).

Holland, J.D., 2009. A Welfare Consensus? Social Policy from Thatcher to Blair. MA thesis, University of Durham. Available from: http://etheses.dur.ac.uk/51/ (accessed 1 July 2010).

Holmsen, J., 2009. Islamism and Gender: A Case Study of the Algerian MSP (HMS). MA thesis, University of Oslo. Available from: www.duo.uio.no/publ/statsvitenskap/2009/97796/Masteroppgave.pdf (accessed 26 March 2011).

Langslet, N., 2008. Subordination, Migration and Mobilization: Strategies for Coping in an Altered Security Situation. MA thesis, University of Oslo. Available from: www.duo.uio.no/publ/iss/2008/75212/Langslet.pdf (accessed 26 March 2011).

Lee, L., 2006. The 'Secular' Individual in Britain: Toward a Sociology of (Ir)religion. MA thesis, University of Cambridge.

Lian, M.H., 2010. Foreign Policy in American Presidential Elections: A Study of Five Presidential Elections Between 1992 and 2008. MA thesis, University of Oslo. Available from: www.duo.uio.no/sok/work.html?WORKID=102711 (accessed 16 April 2011).

Lie, Ø.B. and Bø, R., 2010. The Effects of Acute Tryptophan Depletion on Impulsivity and Mood in Adolescents Engaging in Non-suicidal Self-injury. MA thesis, University of Oslo. Available from: www.duo.uio.no/sok/work.html?WORKID=106391 (accessed 24 April 2011).

Lindviksmoen, S., 2007. Making Sense of Iraq: Debunking the Conventional Wisdom by Looking at the Iraq War from Three Angles. MA thesis, University of Oslo. Available from: www.duo.uio.no/publ/ILOS/2007/59108/Simenlin.pdf (accessed 24 April 2011).

Merton, R.K., 1965. Some notes on problem-formulation in sociology. In R.K. Merton, L. Bloom and L.S. Cottrell, (eds), Sociology Today: Problems and Prospects, Vol. I. New York: Harper & Row, p. ix–xxxiv.

Moosavi, L., 2007. Understanding the Representation of Muslims and Islam in Speeches by the British Government Using Discourse Analysis. MA thesis, Lancaster University.

Nash, S., 2010. Regenerative Practice. MA thesis, Oxford Brookes University.

Revheim, K.L., 2004. The Recycling of Geopolitical Ideas and the Affirmation of Old World Order Theories: An Analysis of Samuel P. Huntington's Theory 'The Clash of Civilizations'. MA thesis, University of Oslo. Available from: www.duo.uio.no/publ/iks/2004/17556/AUTO/17556.pdf (accessed 26 March 2011).

Rudestam, K.E. and Newton, R.R., 2007. Surviving Your Dissertation: A Comprehensive Guide to Content and Process, 3rd edn. London: Sage.

Salinas, C.G., 2010. Wistful Hope: Local Responses to Neo-Liberal Politics: Uruguay and the Pulp Industry. MA thesis, University of Oslo. Available from: www.duo.uio.no/sok/work.html?WORKID=103463 (accessed 12 November 2011).

Siakwah, P., 2010. Microcredit as a Strategy for Poverty Reduction, Youth and Women Empowerment, Ghana. MA thesis, University of Oslo. Available from: www.duo.uio.no/publ/iss/2010/102803/siakwah.pdf (accessed 26 March 2011).

Stakes, R., 2010. Perceptions of Organisational Culture: A Case Study Set Within the Context of Recent Developments in Higher Education. MA thesis, University of Durham. Available from: http://etheses.dur.ac.uk/324/ (accessed 1 July 2012).

Stenbakken, A.T.A., 2007. What Makes a Politician Persuasive? A Study of Ideology, Rhetoric and Modality in Speeches by Tony Blair and George W. Bush. MA thesis, University of Oslo. Available from: www.duo.uio.no/sok/work.html?WORKID=69169 (accessed 23 April 2011).

Susaas, A.E., 2010. Change or Continuity? Becoming a Young Mother in an Argentinean Shantytown. MA thesis, University of Oslo. Available from: www.duo.uio.no/publ/iss/2010/104007/Susaas.pdf (accessed 30 July 2011).

Teddlie, C.B. and Tashakkori, A. (eds), 2008. Foundations of Mixed Methods Research: Integrating Quantitative and Qualitative Approaches in the Social and Behavioral Sciences. Thousand Oaks, CA: Sage.

University Library, 2011. Guide to the Harvard System of Referencing, 3rd edn. Available from: http://libweb.anglia.ac.uk/referencing/files/Harvard_referencing_2011.pdf (accessed 15 July 2012).

Vaage, S., 2010. Treatment, Care and Support for HIV Positive People in Rural South Africa: A Qualitative Study of the Link between Formal and Informal Healthcare. MA thesis, University of Oslo. Available from: www.duo.uio.no/sok/work.html?WORKID=103364 (accessed 23 April 2011).

Vold, E., 2007. Enhancement and Capture of Value: The case of the Venezuelan Petroleum Industry. MA thesis, University of Oslo. Available from: www.duo.uio.no/sok/work.html?WORKID=63909 (accessed 23 April 2011).

Walton, D., 2006. Fundamentals of Critical Argumentation. Cambridge: Cambridge University Press.

Ward, R.R., 2010. An Alternative Approach to Child Rescue: Child Emigration Societies in Birmingham and Manchester, 1870–1914. MA thesis, Durham University. Available from: http://etheses.dur.ac.uk/611/ (accessed 1 July 2012).

Weaver, K., 2010. Arab Americans and Segmented Assimilation: Looking Beyond the Theory to the Reality in the Detroit Metro Area. MA thesis, University of Oslo. Available from: www.duo.uio.no/publ/ILOS/2010/107676/thesis.pdf (accessed 1 July 2012).

Wethal, U.B., 2011. Strategies of Avoidance – Value Chain Reactions in the Durban Clothing Industry. MA thesis, University of Oslo. Available from: www.duo.uio.no/publ/iss/2011/124427/Wethal.pdf (accessed 13 May 2012).

Index

Academia 40
advisor 11–12, 42–43, 111, 148
  relationship 45–46
  responsibilities 42–43
analogies 6
analysis 119–131
  categories 120
  coherence 73, 129
  compare similarities and
    differences 124
  consistency 125
  critical 125
  description 122
  develop the argument 125–128
  interpretation 122
  justify the interpretation 124
  key concepts 120
  organize data 120
  prepare data 120
analytical strategies 50
anonymity 110
appendices 138
arguments 82–86, 125–128
  chaining arguments 84
  counter-arguments 83, 126–127
  evaluating 86
  pro-arguments 83
  reliability 86
  significance 86
  validity 81, 87
archives 65
associations 20–21
assumptions 77, 79, 82, 93, 95
audience 27

Bias-free writing 129
bibliographic database 55
books for sale 52
brainstorming 6, 24, 35

Case study 105
Categories 120
chaining arguments 83
classic thesis structure 136
coherence 73, 100, 122, 129, 146
  between different parts of the
    thesis 74, 100, 122, 146
  between theory and empirical
    facts 74, 122
  logical 87
comparisons 78
  positive and negative 78
  propositions 77
  similarities and differences 124
compulsory writing 31
concepts, define 49
conclusion 133
conference proceedings 57, 65
contents 68, 137
contrasts 95, 125
counter-argument 30, 83, 126
critical analysis 77, 82, 125
  data 125
  literature 77, 82

Data 90, 92, 120–128
  availability 108
  organize 120
  prepare 120

Data *cont.*
 reliability 108
 validity 108
 qualitative 90
 quantitative 90
database 54
 international 55
 social scientific 56–57
data collection 106
 anonymity 110
 availability 108
 ethical considerations 109
 primary data 106
 reliability 108
 sample 107
 secondary data 106
 validity 108
deadline 13, 44, 145
decision making 20
developing a topic 5
dictionary, subject 59
differences, look for 78
documentation 8, 78, 122

Editing 136, 148
 different parts of the thesis 147
electronic search 53
 author 53
 classification number 54
 literature 51
 key word 53
 OPAC 53–54, 61, 63, 65, 140
 title 53
 word in title 53–54
Endnote 69
encyclopedia 58–59
 subject 59
ethics 10–13, 15, 42, 106, 109, 114–115, 118, 138, 146
evaluating 86
 arguments 86
 literature 66

Facebook 39
finding a topic 2
front page 137

Gantt chart 15
generalizations 82

general sentences 32, 41, 45
genre 17

Handbooks 58

Identifying useful literature 66–68
 author's name 67
 bibliography 68
 content 67
 contents list 68
 date of publication 67
 index 68
 journal name 67
 preface 68
 publisher 67
 skim reading 68
 text on back cover 68
 title and subtitle 67
 websites 67
inconsistencies 97
Internet 51–52, 66, 143
 bookstores 70
 electronic search 52
 deep web 51
 search engines 51, 55, 66
interpretation 74, 122, 137, 147
 justify 124
introduction 129, 131, 135, 137, 147

Journals 61
journal articles 62

Key concept 7, 13, 16, 49, 120

Language, bias free 129
library OPAC 53–54, 61, 63, 65, 140
LinkedIn 39
Literature 47, 65, 73, 137, 139, 146
 archives 65
 conference proceedings 65
 different types 58
 dissertations 64
 general encylopaedias 58
 handbooks 58
 journals 61
 journal articles 62
 official publications 64, 70
 official statistics 64, 70
 references 139

Literature *cont.*
  research reports 63
  search 47, 51
  subject dictionaries 59
  subject encyclopaedias 59
  textbooks 63
  theses 64
  use 48
literature review 73, 75
  coherence 74
  critical analysis 77, 82
  describe 75
  discuss 82
  raise questions and critique 77
  theoretical frame 49, 74
logical coherence 87

Manual literature search 54
Mendeley 69
Metalib 54
method, see research method
methods chapter 111–112, 146
mind map 7–8, 16
motivation 21

Networks, academic and professional 39
notes 139

Official publications 64, 70
official statistics 64, 70
OPAC 53–54, 61, 63, 65, 140
overall research questions 92
  contrasts 95
  differences 95
  different types 92
  discovering facts 93
  explaining a phenomenon 93
  observations 98
  patterns 94
  practical rationale 97
  processes 94–95
  rationale 96
  relations between several
    phenomena 93
  specify 98
  theoretical rationale 96

Paragraph 24, 32–35
persuasive writing 30

phenomena, relation between 93
practical consideration in data
    collection 106
preface 68
primary data 106
prioritize 24–25
pro-argument 83, 126
progress 18, 43
project planning 13, 68
proposition 33, 77
  false 79, 83
  true 79, 83
  reliability 86
  significance 77
  questioning 79

Quotations 122, 138

Rationale of the research question 96
  practical 97
  theoretical 96
references 139
  electronic sources 142
  in the text 141
  list of 143
  literature 139
relevant literature 48
reliability 86, 108
  data 108
  arguments 86
research ethics 10–13, 15, 106, 109,
    114–115, 118, 138, 146
research design 102
  data availability 108
  data reliability 108
  data validity 109
  methods 103
  sample of subjects and data 107
research literature 47, 73
  critical analysis 77, 82
  describe 75
  discuss 82
  search 47, 51
  theoretical discussion 49, 74
research findings 122, 126, 134,
    137, 147
research methods 13, 62, 103, 133, 137
  qualitative 103
  quantitative 103

research proposal 11
research report 63
research questions 89
  adjust 92
  descriptive questions 93
  formulate 92
  hypotheses 91
  overall 92
  scientific question 89–90
  specified questions 98
  topic 90
  qualitative 90
  quantitative 90
RSS-feeds 54
results of study 122, 134, 137

Sample 13, 107
  data 107
  subjects 107
searching literature 47
  author 53
  bibliographic database 54
  books for sale 52
  catalogues 52
  databases 54
  electronic search 53
  international databases 55
  Internet 53, 66
  library 52
  key word 53
  manual search 54
  Metalib 54
  OPAC 53–54, 61, 63, 65, 140
  search log 68
  types of literature 58
search log 68
  data files 69
  Endnote 69
  copies 68
  Mendeley 69
  Zotero 69
self-image 20–22
sentences 24, 31, 88, 145
  general 32
  opening 88
  topic 32
similarities 78, 124
skim reading 5, 36, 68

social media 5, 39, 119
  Academia 40
  Facebook 39
  LinkedIn 39
Specify 7, 9, 49
  research topic 7, 9
  research questions 49, 90, 98
statistics 64, 70
strategies for designing a master's
    thesis 104
  case-studies 105
  fill gaps in previous research 104
  reappraise previous research 105
  repeat previous research 105
  write a thesis within the frames of
      a research program 106
structure 31, 33, 119, 137
  analysis 119
  paragraph 33
  sentence 31
  thesis 137
students 40, 42
  networks 40,
  responsibilities 42
summary 134
  conclusions 134
  findings 134
  results from the study 134

Textbooks 63
topic 1
  find 2
  decision 9
  develop 5
  distance to 3
  research ethics 10
theoretical framework 49
theoretical assumptions 82, 95
theoretical discussion 124
thesis structure 136
tricks to continue writing 35

Uninvited writing 31
unpublished material 65

Validity 81, 87, 109
  argument 81, 87
  data 109

Visualization 22

Websites 67
writing
　assessing skills 24, 26
　bias-free 129
　compulsory 31
　ethics 129
　hindrances for 18
　motivation 21
　persuasive 30
　practice 35
　purpose 29

writing *cont.*
　routines 23
　rules 27
　structure 31
　styles 30
　tricks to continue 35
　uninvited 31
writing blocks 18
　emotional and cognitive 18
　task blocks 19
writing styles 30

Zotero 69